BAZI STRUCTURES

&

Structural Useful Gods

WOOD 木

甲 Jia
乙 Yi

格局與格局用神

BaZi Structures & Structural Useful Gods
Wood Structure

The author can be reached at:

Mastery Academy of Chinese Metaphysics Sdn. Bhd. (611143-A)
19-3, The Boulevard, Mid Valley City,
59200 Kuala Lumpur, Malaysia.
Tel   : +603-2284 8080
Fax   : +603-2284 1218
Email   : info@masteryacademy.com
Website: www.masteryacademy.com

DISCLAIMER:

Published by JY Books Sdn. Bhd. (659134-T)

Table of Contents

Jia 甲 Wood Day Master, Born in :

Table of Contents

Yi 乙 Wood Day Master, Born in :

About The Chinese Metaphysics Reference Series

Reference Series

The Chinese Metaphysics Reference Series of books are designed primarily to be used as complimentary textbooks for scholars, students, researchers, teachers and practitioners of Chinese Metaphysics.

The goal is to provide quick easy reference tables, diagrams and charts, facilitating the study and practice of various Chinese Metaphysics subjects including Feng Shui, BaZi, Yi Jing, Zi Wei, Liu Ren, Ze Ri, Ta Yi, Qi Men and Mian Xiang.

This series of books are intended as <u>reference text and educational materials</u> principally for the academic syllabuses of the **Mastery Academy of Chinese Metaphysics**. The contents have also been formatted so that Feng Shui Masters and other teachers of Chinese Metaphysics will always have a definitive source of reference at hand, when teaching or applying their art.

Because each school of Chinese Metaphysics is different, the Reference Series of books usually do not contain any specific commentaries, application methods or explanations on the theory behind the formulas presented in its contents. This is to ensure that the contents can be used freely and independently by all Feng Shui Masters and teachers of Chinese Metaphysics without conflict.

If you would like to study or learn the applications of any of the formulas presented in the Reference Series of books, we recommend that you undertake the courses offered by Joey Yap and his team of Instructors at the Mastery Academy of Chinese Metaphysics.

Titles offers in the Reference Series:

1. The Chinese Metaphysics Compendium
2. Dong Gong Date Selection
3. Earth Study Discern Truth
4. Xuan Kong Da Gua Structure Reference Book
5. San Yuan Dragon Gate Eight Formations Water Method
6. Xuan Kong Da Gua Ten Thousand Year Calendar
7. Plum Blossom Divination Reference Book
8. The Date Selection Compendium (Book 1) - The 60 Jia Zi Attributes
9. BaZi Structures & Structural Useful Gods Reference Series

Preface

The study and practice of BaZi is an infinitely rewarding and intriguing one, with literally an inexhaustible depth and range from which we can mine our information on a person's character, temperament, life outlook and personal destiny. The simplest data – your birth date and time – can yield a rich treasure trove of knowledge, most of which can help shed new light on old perceptions.

The idea for this BaZi Structures and Structural Useful God Reference Series came out of a common need among my BaZi students, many of whom wanted to learn more about how the various structures in BaZi are derived. This series was therefore created to help students learn and absorb the methods and techniques in which a structure is created and developed mainly from a classical standpoint.

While initially it was my idea to create one BaZi Structures book to accommodate all 10 Heavenly Stems (Day Masters), I soon found out that it would not be a book that could reasonably be used by anyone – because it would be too heavy to lift! So I decided to break it apart into five different books, with each one corresponding to each Element. The book you're holding in your hands is on Wood Structures, for both Jia 甲 and Yi 乙 Wood Day Masters.

There are many traditional sources available on the BaZi structures, and the derivation of those structures. One of the more well-known texts is the *Qiong Tong Bao Jian* 窮通寶鑑, written by a famous master, *Xu Le Wu* 徐樂吾. Another popular BaZi scholar of recent past who contributed a lot to mainstream BaZi theories, especially those relating to structures, is *Wei Qian Li* 韋千里.

It's difficult for most students to have access to this information because it's scattered about in various texts and documents, and also – all of it is available only in Chinese. It was my intention, therefore, to compile this information into one convenient source, and to present the transliterated version of these traditional texts for the modern, English-speaking practitioner and student without losing the essence of the original.

To derive a structure and structural Useful God in BaZi, one must know and understand the Day Master and the month of birth, and its variations in a BaZi chart. There are traditional methods on how this is derived, and there are newer interpretations on these methods.

As such, different practitioners and teachers have different methods and formats to derive these structures, and it is recommended that you use the techniques outlined in this book with care and thought. As always, there is much merit in using traditional practices, but students who are learning BaZi should use this under the supervision of a teacher in order to better understand the subject. A good teacher will help you understand the different ways of interpreting these traditional texts.

Do note that these texts should not be taken literally. Different masters may agree or disagree with the classical commentaries included here, and as a student, it's important for you to know the reasons why. Better yet, it's important for you to know those reasons and then go on to form your own conclusions, based on your understanding of the various interpretations.

For that reason, this book was designed to be a reference accompaniment for the students of my BaZi Mastery Series, where you'll be able to get the guidance you need in interpreting these traditional methods. I encourage you to take a class because it will help to place this material in context and give you the added knowledge you need to help you make the most of the information contained within this book. Each and every structure in this book could be its own chapter, because it can literally explain a person and his or her modus operandi!

I hope you enjoy your research on this subject, and here's to many pleasurable hours of BaZi Structural study!

Warm regards,

Joey Yap
July 2009

Author's personal websites :
www.joeyyap.com

Academy websites :
www.masteryacademy.com | www.masteryjournal.com | www.maelearning.com

Follow Joey's current updates on Twitter :
www.twitter.com/joeyyap

Get to know Joey on Facebook :
www.facebook.com/joeyyapFB

MASTERY ACADEMY
OF CHINESE METAPHYSICS™

At **www.masteryacademy.com**, you will find some useful tools to ascertain key information about the Feng Shui of a property or for the study of Astrology.

The Joey Yap Flying Stars Calculator can be utilised to plot your home or office Flying Stars chart. To find out your personal best directions, use the 8 Mansions Calculator. To learn more about your personal Destiny, you can use the Joey Yap BaZi Ming Pan Calculator to plot your Four Pillars of Destiny – you just need to have your date of birth (day, month, year) and time of birth.

For more information about BaZi, Xuan Kong or Flying Star Feng Shui, or if you wish to learn more about these subjects with Joey Yap, logon to the Mastery Academy of Chinese Metaphysics website at **www.masteryacademy.com.**

www.maelearning.com

Bookmark this address on your computer, and visit this newly-launched website today. With the E-Learning Center, knowledge of Chinese Metaphysics is a mere 'click' away!

Our E-Learning Center consists of 3 distinct components.

1. Online Courses
These shall comprise of 3 Programs: our Online Feng Shui Program, Online BaZi Program, and Online Mian Xiang Program. Each lesson contains a video lecture, slide presentation and downloadable course notes.

2. MA Live!
With MA Live!, Joey Yap's workshops, tutorials, courses and seminars on various Chinese Metaphysics subjects broadcasted right to your computer screen. Better still, participants will not only get to see and hear Joey talk 'live', but also get to engage themselves directly in the event and more importantly, TALK to Joey via the MA Live! interface. All the benefits of a live class, minus the hassle of actually having to attend one!

3. Video-On-Demand (VOD)
Get immediate streaming-downloads of the Mastery Academy's wide range of educational DVDs, right on your computer screen. No more shipping costs and waiting time to be incurred!

Study at your own pace, and interact with your Instructor and fellow students worldwide… at your own convenience and privacy. With our E-Learning Center, knowledge of Chinese Metaphysics is brought DIRECTLY to you in all its clarity, with illustrated presentations and comprehensive notes expediting your learning curve!

Welcome to the Mastery Academy's E-LEARNING CENTER…YOUR virtual gateway to Chinese Metaphysics mastery!

Introduction - Wood Day Masters

As with the rest of the Five Elements, there are 2 types of Wood Day Masters: Jia 甲 Wood and Yi 乙 Wood.

Anyone who has seen a piece of Wood would surely be able to tell that it is usually straight and unchanging. After all, when was the last time one saw a piece of Wood that was curved – unless it has become warped, in which case, it would not be a good piece of Wood?

Unsurprisingly, Wood people tend to be rather set in their ways and habits. Nevertheless, they can also be sentimental at heart – just as trees, including little weeds, usually never stray far from where they are planted, seeded or take root. This is indeed true to the saying that the `acorn never falls far from the oak'.

Wood people hence often need to stay in and remain rooted to the same spot. In other words, Wood Day Masters like stability and dislike to be uprooted or moved about. It is this rooting though that gives them their steadfast attitude and diehard perseverance, and they will usually find at least some small measure of success in their lives. Determined and progressive as they may be, the efforts and progress of Wood Day Masters may not be obvious, but then again, just because we rarely see trees or plants grow does not mean that they are not growing at all.

Of course, these are the general characteristics of Wood Day Masters – although the manifestations and magnitude of these characteristics can still differ, depending on whether it's a Jia (Yang) Wood Day Master or Yi (Yin) Wood Day Master we are dealing with.

Nevertheless, there are certain key qualities or attributes that can be deduced, once we identify whether a Wood Day Master is a Jia Wood or Yi Wood Day Master. Jia Wood types are usually steady, forthright, direct, stern, straightforward and sturdy. Some of their more negative attributes, though, include the tendency to be stubborn and slow to act.

Yi Wood types, meanwhile, tend to be more flexible and adaptable to changing circumstances, compared to their Jia Wood counterparts. They are also good motivators; although true to their Yin nature, they can be just as fickle and show-offish, if the mood strikes them.

Jia (甲) Wood Day Master

Overview:

Being Yang Wood, Jia 甲 Wood represents hard, enduring types of Wood; such as the large, looming trees commonly found forests and jungles throughout the world.

True to the laws of nature, Jia Wood is most significantly affected by the presence – or lack thereof – of sunlight and moisture. Nevertheless, the outcomes and circumstances for Jia Wood Day Masters vary greatly; depending on their season or month of birth.

Jia Wood types are – in a nutshell - usually steady, forthright, direct, stern, straightforward and sturdy by nature – although they can also be stubborn, slow to act and hold extremely conservative views towards life.

Jia 甲 Wood Day Master, Born in First Month 正月

Yin 寅 (Tiger) Month
February 4th – March 5th

Do note that the dates provided above are subject to slight yearly variations. Please refer to the Ten Thousand Year Calendar for the accurate transition dates for each year.

Day Master Jia 甲 Wood | **Month** Yin 寅 (Tiger)

日元 **Day Master**	月 **Month**

甲
Jia
Yang Wood

寅
Yin
Tiger
Yang Wood

For a Jia Wood Day Master born in a Yin (Tiger) Month, the Earthly Branch of Yin (Tiger) is Jia Wood's 'Prosperous' position; this usually results in a Thriving Structure being formed.

Where Jia Wood is revealed as one of the Heavenly Stems, a Thriving Structure is definitely formed.

Where Bing Fire is revealed as one of the Heavenly Stems, an Eating God Structure may be formed when the conditions are completely met and supported by the Earthly branches.

Where Wu Earth is revealed as one of the Heavenly Stems, an Indirect Wealth Structure may be formed when the conditions are completely met and supported by the Earthly branches.

Day Master Jia 甲 Wood   **Month** Yin 寅 (Tiger)

喜用神提要 **Regulating Useful God Reference Guide**

月 Month	用神 Useful God

1st Month 正月
Yin 寅 (Tiger) Month

丙
Bing
Yang Fire

癸
Gui
Yin Water

For a Yin (Tiger) Month, Bing Fire and Gui Water are its Regulating Useful Gods.

Bing Fire is this Day Master's primary Useful God, while Gui Water serves as its secondary Useful God.

正
月
First Month

寅
Tiger

5

| Day Master Jia 甲 Wood | Month Yin 寅 (Tiger) |

4th day of February – 5th day of March, Gregorian Calendar

Given that a Yin (Tiger) Month signals the transition between winter and spring, Jia Wood is invariably 'stuck' (or cold) at this time of the year. The cold needs to be treated in order for Wood to grow.

Fire is needed to provide 'warmth' to this Day Master; given that it is still very cold at this time of the year. The importance of Fire cannot be underestimated, since it also governs the quality of this Day Master's wealth luck and prospects in life.

To put things into perspective, the ability of Fire to produce Earth – this Day Master's Wealth Star – will influence the outcomes of this Day Master's capacity and potential in life.

Day Master	Jia 甲 Wood	Month	Yin 寅 (Tiger)

正
月
First Month

Tiger

Commentary

In addition to the preceding narratives on the potential Structures and scenarios resulting from a Jia Wood Day Master born in a Yin (Tiger) Month, the following circumstances also play their respective roles in determining the overall strength of this Day Master's BaZi Chart.

Note:

• Where Bing Fire and Gui Water are both revealed in the Heavenly Stems, this Day Master shall enjoy excellent career and wealth luck.

• Even if Gui Water remains hidden within the Earthly Branches – instead of being revealed in the Heavenly Stems – this Day Master shall still be blessed with good wealth luck in life, but lack nobility.

• A mediocre, average Day Master would be the outcome, where Gui Water is completely missing from the chart – while Bing Fire is also not revealed in the Heavenly Stems.

• It would also be unfavorable to this Day Master, where Ren Water and Ji Earth are revealed in the Heavenly Stems.

• Bing Fire is extremely important as a Regulating Useful God to this Day Master, especially in a Yin (Tiger) Month, since it counters the chill and cold that are still prevalent at this time of the year. Bing Fire would still interact with and counter Metal, if present, in the BaZi Chart.

• Given that Jia Wood is firmly 'rooted' in the Yin (Tiger) Earthly Branch's main Hidden Stem, a Thriving Structure is formed in the BaZi Chart. Given its strength, it would be impossible for a Follow the Wealth, Follow the Killings or any Transforming Structure to be formed.

• It would be unfavorable to have Earth (Wealth Star) present in abundance. Too much Earth will not foster good growth of the Wood element in this month.

• Where Geng Metal or Xin Metal is revealed in the Heavenly Stems – but Bing Fire and Ding Fire happen to be missing – this Day Master may have to struggle and slog in life, in order to make a living. His or her relationship luck with loved ones will also be poor, while he or she will also suffer from poverty and poor health.

• Where Bing Fire or Ding Fire is revealed in the Heavenly Stems – together with Gui Water – this Day Master shall prosper and become very wealthy in life. Without Gui Water, this Day Master may only be able to lead an average life; no matter how diligent and hardworking he or she may be.

| **Day Master** Jia 甲 Wood | **Month** Yin 寅 (Tiger) |

- Where Ren Water or Gui Water is revealed in the Heavenly Stems, the Bing Fire as a Regulating Useful God must be present and unobstructed. If this is attainable, this Day Master shall be a skillful, talented one.

- Where an additional Jia Wood or Yi Wood is revealed in the Heavenly Stems, there must be at one strong and rooted Geng Metal Heavenly Stems present. Otherwise, this Day Master may lack a sense of purpose or direction in life; no matter how learned or knowledgeable he or she may be.

- Where Wu Earth or Ji Earth is revealed in the Heavenly Stems, Geng Metal (Seven Killings Star) would be produced and strengthened by the presence of Earth. Under such circumstances, however, this Day Master may be predisposed towards squandering his or her wealth away, especially on frivolous or lascivious pursuits.

- Where Bing Fire or Ding Fire is revealed in the Heavenly Stems, this Day Master shall belong to an extremely skillful or talented person. Nevertheless, because Fire weakens this Jia Wood Day Master, he or she may also be susceptible to poor health and illness in life.

- Where Jia Wood or Yi Wood is revealed – while Wu Earth and Ji Earth also penetrate to the Heavenly Stems – this Day Master shall enjoy good wealth luck in life. Without Gui Water, though, he or she may possess a stubborn or obstinate personality.

- Where Wu Earth or Ji Earth are revealed in the Heavenly Stems, the presence of Ding Fire (this Day Master's Hurting Officer Star) will result in Earth Qi (Wealth Star) being supported. Where Ding Fire is present, Gui Water should not be missing – otherwise, this Day Master may still be afflicted by poverty; even if he or she comes from an affluent household.

- Where Geng Metal or Xin Metal is revealed in the Heavenly Stems, there would be a surplus of elements that serve to control and weaken this Day Master. Where this is seen, this Day Master shall possess an obstinate, stubborn personality, which would cause him or her much conflict with others. He or she will also find it difficult to amass or accumulate wealth in life.

- Where Ren Water or Gui Water is revealed in the Heavenly Stems, a situation analogous to Wood 'floating' on or 'washed away' by Water takes place. Under such circumstances, this Day Master may suffer from poverty in life; regardless of how skillful or talented he or she may be.

- Where Jia Wood or Yi Wood is revealed in the Heavenly Stems – while a Water or Wood Structure is formed – this Day Master will never be in want of friends, throughout his or her entire life.

Day Master Jia 甲 Wood   **Month** Yin 寅 (Tiger)

- Where Geng Metal or Xin Metal is revealed in the Heavenly Stems – while Water (Resource Star) is present – this Day Master shall be blessed with a high level of authority or status in life.

- Where Bing Fire or Ding Fire is revealed in the Heavenly Stems, the presence of Ding Fire (Hurting Officer Star) and Water Qi (Resource Star) would allow this Day Master to be blessed with a high level of authority or status in life.

- Where Jia Wood or Yi Wood is revealed in the Heavenly Stems – while this Day Master's BaZi Chart consists of Wood Stars entirely – Geng Metal must also be seen in the Heavenly Stems. Otherwise, this Day Master may be afflicted by loneliness and constant frustrations in life.

- Where Wu Earth or Ji Earth is revealed in the Heavenly Stems - the abundance of Earth (Wealth Star) would invariably weaken this Jia Wood Day Master. Consequently, this person may be so inclined towards pursuing wealth, to the extent that he or she may neglect everything and everyone else.

- Where Bing Fire or Ding Fire is revealed in the Heavenly Stems – while there is at least one of the Four Graveyard Earthly Branches of Chen (Dragon), Xu (Dog), Chou (Ox) or Wei (Goat) present – this Day Master shall be able to prosper and become wealthy in life.

- Where Ren Water or Gui Water is revealed in the Heavenly Stems, this Day Master may possess a fickle-minded personality. In addition, his or her ability to achieve fame and fortune in life may also be extremely limited due to inability to be decisive.

- Where Wu Earth or Ji Earth is revealed in the Heavenly Stems, the abundant presence of Earth (Wealth Star) would result in Water (Resource Star) falling under the former's control. Consequently, this Day Master may prosper in life; although he or she may also be incapable of enjoying what life has to offer. There would be discontentment.

- Where Geng Metal or Xin Metal is revealed in the Heavenly Stems, the presence of Earth (Wealth Star) would invariably lead to Geng Metal (Seven Killings Star) being supported. Under such circumstances, though, this Day Master may be plagued by disharmony on the domestic front, due to wealth or money-related matters and disputes.

- Where Bing Fire or Ding Fire is revealed in the Heavenly Stems, the presence of Bing Fire (Eating God Star) or Ding Fire (Hurting Officer Star) would lead to Earth Qi (Wealth Star) being produced. Under such circumstances, this Day Master may possess a superficial personality or be prone towards assuming appearances.

| **Day Master** Jia 甲 Wood | **Month** Yin 寅 (Tiger) |

Additional Attributes

格局 **Structural Star**	食神 Eating God	正印 Direct Resource
用神 **Useful God**	Bing 丙 Fire	Gui 癸 Water
Conditions	If neither Bing Fire nor Gui Water forms its relevant structure with this Day Master, he or she may not be able to prosper in life.	
Positive Circumstances	Bing Fire and Gui Water revealed in the Heavenly Stems	
Negative Circumstances	Absence of Bing Fire or Gui Water.	

格局 **Structural Star**	七殺 Seven Killings	正官 Direct Officer
用神 **Useful God**	Geng 庚 Metal	Xin 辛 Metal
Conditions	Where neither Bing Fire nor Ding Fire is revealed in the Heavenly Stems, this Day Master may not be blessed with prosperity and longevity in life. This Day Master may have to slog or toil throughout his or her entire life to make a living. His or her relationship luck will also be poor, with male Day Masters possibly experiencing a tense relationship with their wives and sons.	
Positive Circumstances	Where Bing Fire forms an Eating God Structure or Ding Fire forms a Hurting Officer Structure with this Day Master.	
Negative Circumstances	Neither Bing Fire nor Ding Fire is revealed in the Heavenly Stems. Without either, this Day Master would be without support or assistance.	

Day Master Jia 甲 Wood   **Month** Yin 寅 (Tiger)

Additional Attributes

格局 **Structural Star**	偏印 Indirect Resource	正印 Direct Resource
用神 **Useful God**	Ren 壬 Water	Gui 癸 Water
Conditions	Where the Earthly Branches forms a Resource Structure fin the BaZi Chart – and while Bing Fire is not revealed in the Heavenly Stems – this Day Master may be afflicted by poverty in life.	
Positive Circumstances	Wu Earth (Indirect Wealth Star) and Ji Earth (Direct Wealth Star) penetrate to the Heavenly Stems.	
Negative Circumstances	Without Bing Fire (Eating God Star) revealed in the Heavenly Stems, this Day Master would be without help or support.	

格局 **Structural Star**	偏財 Indirect Wealth	正財 Direct Wealth
用神 **Useful God**	Wu 戊 Earth	Ji 己 Earth
Conditions	Where Earth forms a full Wealth Structure with this Day Master, there is a need to avoid having an abundance of any of the following Earthly Branches: Shen (Monkey), You (Rooster), Chou (Ox) and Xu (Dog).	
Positive Circumstances	Only Bing Fire is seen penetrating to the Heavenly Stems.	
Negative Circumstances	Geng Metal and Xin Metal are revealed, as well as penetrate to the Heavenly Stems.	

正
月

First Month

寅

Tiger

11

Day Master Jia 甲 Wood		**Month** Yin 寅 (Tiger)

Additional Attributes

格局 **Structural Star**	七殺 Seven Killings	傷官 Hurting Officer
用神 **Useful God**	Geng 庚 Metal	Ding 丁 Fire
Conditions	Where Geng Metal is present in abundance, Ding Fire is also needed, in order to enhance this Day Master's luck and fortunes in life by forging the Geng Metal. Where Ding Fire is present in abundance, Geng Metal is needed in order to bring about the same outcomes.	
Positive Circumstances	Where there is one Geng Metal Heavenly Stem present, at least one Ding Fire should also be seen.	
Negative Circumstances	Where Ding Fire is used, without Geng Metal, there is a need to avoid having Gui Water (Direct Resource Star) penetrating to the Heavenly Stems.	

格局 **Structural Star**	食神 Eating God	傷官 Hurting Officer
用神 **Useful God**	Bing 丙 Fire	Ding 丁 Fire
Conditions	Where an Eating God or Hurting Officer Structure is formed, it would also be necessary for Ren Water and Gui Water – Resource Stars – to be seen penetrating to the Heavenly Stems.	
Positive Circumstances	Ren Water and Gui Water must also penetrate to the Heavenly Stems. Otherwise, this Day Master may lack intelligence, as well as be susceptible to poor health and illness in life.	
Negative Circumstances	Ren Water and Gui Water (Resource Stars) do not penetrate to the Heavenly Stems.	

Day Master Jia 甲 Wood   **Month** Yin 寅 (Tiger)

Additional Attributes

格局 Structural Star	七殺 Seven Killings	正官 Direct Officer
用神 Useful God	Geng 庚 Metal	Xin 辛 Metal
Conditions	Where a Direct Officer or Seven Killings Structure is formed, Bing Fire and Ding Fire must be selected as Useful Gods. Otherwise, this Day Master may be afflicted by physical disability and poor health in life.	
Positive Circumstances	Bing Fire and Ding Fire also penetrate to the Heavenly Stems.	
Negative Circumstances	Gui Water (Direct Resource Star) penetrates to the Heavenly Stems, as well.	

格局 Structural Star	偏印 Indirect Resource	正印 Direct Resource
用神 Useful God	Ren 壬 Water	Gui 癸 Water
Conditions	Water is not preferred to be producing Wood (this Day Master), in the springtime. Where a Resource Structure is formed– without Wu Earth also present – this Day Master may be afflicted by poverty or at least, immense obstacles in life.	
Positive Circumstances	Even if Wu Earth is available, Bing Fire must also be revealed in the Heavenly Stems. Where Wu Earth (Indirect Wealth Star) penetrates to the Heavenly Stems, it would not be possible for there to be any support forthcoming from Ji Earth, if present – unless and until Bing Fire (Eating God Star) is also seen.	
Negative Circumstances	Neither Wu Earth nor Bing Fire penetrates to the Heavenly Stems.	

* *Bing Fire and Gui Water are the preferred Useful Gods for a Jia Wood Day Master born in a Yin (Tiger) Month.*

* *Geng Metal and Ding Fire are also the preferred Useful Gods for a Jia Wood Day Master born in a Yin (Tiger) Month.*

13

| Day Master | Jia 甲 Wood | | Month | Yin 寅 (Tiger) |

正月 First Month

寅 Tiger

Summary

- Where the Yin (Tiger), Mao (Rabbit) and Chen (Dragon) Earthly Branches form a Wood Structure, Geng Metal (a Seven Killings Star) remains an important Useful God, in keeping Wood under control.

- Where Water forms a Resource Structure with this Day Master, there would be no need to avoid having Earth (Wealth Star) keeping Water under control.

- Where Earth forms a Wealth Structure with this Day Master – while Xin Metal (Direct Officer Star) and Geng Metal (Seven Killings Star) are also revealed – this Day Master's BaZi Chart would be of a substandard structure. It is unfavorable to have strong Earth (Wealth Star) producing even more Metal (Officer Star).

- Even without Geng Metal, Ding Fire (Hurting Officer Star) may still be used to weaken this Day Master to a certain extent and hence keep it well-balanced.

- Should neither Geng Metal nor Ding Fire happen to be available as Useful Gods, this Day Master may still prosper and thrive; provided it encounters Wu Earth or Ji Earth.

Jia 甲 Wood Day Master, Born in Second Month 二月

Mao 卯 (Rabbit) Month
March 6th – April 4th

Do note that the dates provided above are subject to slight yearly variations. Please refer to the Ten Thousand Year Calendar for the accurate transition dates for each year.

| Day Master | Jia 甲 Wood | Month | Mao 卯 (Rabbit) |

日元 Day Master	月 Month
甲 *Jia* **Yang Wood**	卯 *Mao* **Rabbit** **Yin Wood**

For a Jia Wood Day Master born in a Mao (Rabbit) Month, a
Goat Blade Structure would be formed between the Mao (Rabbit)
Earthly Branch and this Day Master.

Day Master Jia 甲 Wood   **Month** Mao 卯 (Rabbit)

喜用神提要 **Regulating Useful God Reference Guide**

月 **Month**	用神 **Useful God**

2nd Month 二月
Mao 卯 (Rabbit) Month

庚 *Geng* **Yang Metal**   丙 *Bing* **Yang Fire**   丁 *Ding* **Yin Fire**   戊 *Wu* **Yang Earth**   己 *Ji* **Yin Earth**

For a Mao (Rabbit) Month, Geng Metal, Bing Fire, Ding Fire, Wu Earth and Ji Earth are its Regulating Useful Gods.

The formation of a Goat Blade Structure also brings about Sha (Killing) Qi. This is why Wu Earth and Ji Earth are required as Useful Gods, in suppressing this indomitable Qi.

In the absence of Geng Metal, Bing Fire and Ding Fire may also be used to weaken this Day Master to a certain extent – and hence keep balanced. It would indeed be preferable to weaken – instead of control – the Killing Qi.

Day Master   Jia 甲 Wood   Month   Mao 卯 (Rabbit)

6th day of March – 4th day of April, Gregorian Calendar

For this Day Master, the Earthly Branch of Mao (Rabbit) is also Jia Wood's Goat Blade position. In other words, Wood is firmly 'rooted', and therefore extremely prosperous.

Fire produces Earth, which is this Day Master's Wealth Star.

Metal is needed to 'shape' and make this Jia Wood Day Master more 'appealing'. If this is attainable, male Day Masters – in particular – shall be blessed with a very high status and authority in life.

Likewise, Metal is needed in the case of female Day Masters, if they are to enjoy good relationship luck with their spouse.

Day Master Jia 甲 Wood **Month** Mao 卯 (Rabbit)

Commentary

In addition to the preceding narratives on the potential Structures and scenarios resulting from a Jia Wood Day Master born in a Mao (Rabbit) Month, the following circumstances also play their respective roles in determining the overall strength of this Day Master's BaZi Chart.

Note:

- A Goat Blade Structure is invariably formed in this BaZi Chart.

- It would be undesirable to have Gui Water.

- Geng Metal and Ding Fire are this Day Master's preferred Regulating Useful Gods.

- In order to produce a good quality, strong, thriving Jia Wood Day Master, Geng Metal is the primary Regulating Useful God.

- In the absence of Geng Metal, Ding Fire may be used to weaken this Day Master and ensure it's balance.

- Jia Wood should not be parted from Geng Metal, just as Geng Metal should not be seen without Ding Fire. This is the law of interdependence.

- Any Day Master that employs Geng Metal as a Useful God should not be missing Ding Fire, either. This is because without Ding Fire, Geng Metal is powerless.

- It is undesirable to have Bing Fire and Gui Water penetrate to the Heavenly Stems.

- This is because while Ding Fire has the capacity to counter and weaken Geng Metal, Gui Water in turn counters and weakens Ding Fire – whilst simultaneously weakening Geng Metal as well.

- Geng Metal (Seven Killings Star) and Water (Resource Star) should not be simultaneously seen for this Day Master this month. Otherwise this chart would be substandard and inferior.

- It would be impossible for a Follow the Killings Structure to be formed this month.

- The Absence of Geng Metal would mean the person is lacking in substance, wisdome and happiness in life – regardless of how cultured or genteel he or she may be.

- In the absence of Geng Metal, Xin Metal may be used to replace it. Nevertheless, under such circumstances, this Day Master may be predisposed towards making quick – as opposed to long-term, sustainable – gains in life.

- The theories pertaining to the formation of structures and meeting of certain elements for this Day Master are similar as those pertaining to Jia Wood born in a Yin (Tiger) Month.

Day Master Jia 甲 Wood	**Month** Mao 卯 (Rabbit)

Additional Attributes

格局 **Structural Star**	羊刃 Goat Blade
用神 **Useful God**	Geng 庚 Metal
Conditions	Where a Goat Blade Structure is accompanied by a Geng Metal (Seven Killings Star), and a Ding Fire (Hurting Officer Star) - this Day Master stands to enjoy great power, authority and fame. The person would be a very capable leader and enjoy the respect of the public.
Positive Circumstances	Geng Metal and Ding Fire penetrated to the Heavenly Stems.
Negative Circumstances	Where Gui Water (Direct Resource Star) penetrates to the Heavenly Stems, it would counter and hinder the application of this Day Master's Useful Gods. Under such circumstances, this Day Master would possess a ruthless, uncouth personality.

* *Geng Metal, Wu Earth and Ding Fire are the preferred Useful Gods for a Jia Wood Day Master born in a Mao (Rabbit) Month.*

Day Master Jia 甲 Wood	**Month** Mao 卯 (Rabbit)

Summary

- There are two conditions or circumstances that are deemed unfavorable, as far as this Day Master is concerned.
  - The first circumstance is where Bing Fire (Eating God Star) exerts a strong but only surface level control over Geng Metal (Seven Killings Star).
  - The second circumstance is when both this Day Master's Seven Killings (Geng Metal) and Resource (Water) Stars are simultaneously present.

Rabbit

- Should scenario be seen, then this BaZi is a substandard, inferior structure. It denotes a ruthless and uncouth personality. He /she will always seek quick gains at the expense of friendship.

- It would only be good to have Earth (this Day Master's Wealth Star) to support Geng Metal (a Seven Killings Star). But not too much.

- Geng Metal should be used in tandem with Ding Fire. Where this is present, this Goat Blade Structure would be able to exert it's highest level of influence and power. However, the trick here is, both Geng and Ding must be equally strong. Neither one can overpower the other.

Jia 甲 Wood Day Master, Born in Third Month 三月

Chen 辰 (Dragon) Month
April 5th - May 5th

Do note that the dates provided above are subject to slight yearly variations. Please refer to the Ten Thousand Year Calendar for the accurate transition dates for each year.

Day Master Jia 甲 Wood   **Month** Chen 辰 (Dragon)

日元 **Day Master**	月 **Month**

Jia
Yang Wood

Chen
Dragon
Yang Earth

For a Jia Wood Day Master born in a Chen (Dragon) Month, an Indirect Wealth Structure is formed where Wu Earth is revealed as one of the Heavenly Stems.

Where Gui Water is revealed as one of the Heavenly Stems, a Direct Resource Structure is formed.

Where Yi Wood is revealed as one of the Heavenly Stems, a Thriving Structure may be formed when the conditions are completely met and supported by the Earthly branches.

Should, however, neither Wu Earth, Yi Wood nor Gui Water happen to be revealed within the Heavenly Stems, one should select a Structure according to the BaZi Chart's most prominent Qi attribute at one's discretion.

Day Master Jia 甲 Wood   **Month** Chen 辰 (Dragon)

喜用神提要 **Regulating Useful God Reference Guide**

月 **Month**	用神 **Useful God**

3rd Month 三月
Chen 辰 **(Dragon) Month**

Geng
Yang Metal

Ding
Yin Fire

Ren
Yang Water

Dragon

For a Chen (Dragon) Month, Geng Metal, Ding Fire and Ren Water are its most important Regulating Useful Gods.

Where Geng Metal is employed as a Useful God, it must be accompanied by Ding Fire. Without Ding Fire, Geng Metal would not be under control and will not be forged into useful Metal.

In the absence of Geng Metal, Ren Water may be used instead.

Day Master Jia 甲 Wood   Month Chen 辰 (Dragon)
5th day of April – 5th day of May, Gregorian Calendar

The Chen (Dragon) Earthly Branch contains Wu Earth as one of its Hidden Stems. And Earth is this Day Master's Wealth Star.

As such, Water is an essential Useful God, since it provides 'moisture' to this Day Master.

Wood is still very prominently in a Chen (Dragon) Month. This is why Metal should be used to 'carve' and make Wood 'useable', in order for it to be really strong.

Where Metal is present in the BaZi Charts of female Day Masters, they shall be able to enjoy prosperity and good marriage in life. They are likely to attract and marry wealthy as well as loving husbands.

Day Master Jia 甲 Wood　　　　　**Month** Chen 辰 (Dragon)

Commentary

In addition to the preceding narratives on the potential Structures and scenarios resulting from a Jia Wood Day Master born in a Chen (Dragon) Month, the following circumstances also play their respective roles in determining the overall strength of this Day Master's BaZi Chart.

Note:

- Wood Qi is merely beginning to enter the 'wanning' or 'retreating' stage in a Chen (Dragon) Month. This is why Ding Fire alone would be an unsuitable Useful God to this Day Master.

- Geng Metal and Ren Water are the preferred Useful Gods for this Day Master.

- It is undesirable for Ding Fire to be seen penetrating to the Heavenly Stems.

- Where a Wealth Structure is formed, it would be ideal to have either another Jia Wood (Friend Star) or Yi Wood (Rob Wealth Star revealed in the Heavenly stems.

- Should Jia Wood (Friend Star) or Yi Wood (Rob Wealth Star) not to be rooted within the Earthly Branches, this Day Master may tend to possess a 'soft' or gentle or very amicable personality – and as such, possibly even be dominated by their wives. On the other hand, female Day Masters will tend to possess dominant characters and invariably wield a higher level of authority, compared to their male counterparts.

- Where Jia Wood (Friend Star) and Yi Wood (Rob Wealth Star) happen to be rooted as the main qi within several of the Earthly Branches, this Day Master – regardless of male or female – may come from disharmonious or even dysfunctional families.

- Ding Fire should not penetrate to the Heavenly Stems, where Geng Metal and Ren Water are employed as Useful Gods to this Day Master.

- This is because Ding Fire will invariably exert a strong control over Geng Metal and weaken it accordingly. Ding Fire also combines with Ren Water to form Wood. In other words, Ding Fire would negate the beneficial effects brought about Geng Metal and Ren Water should it appear in the Heavenly Stems.

- The only way to negate or counter the influence of Ding Fire – where present – is by having an abundance of Geng Metal (Seven Killings Star) present, as well as either Geng Metal or Xin Metal revealed within the Heavenly Stems.

27

| Day Master | Jia 甲 Wood | Month | Chen 辰 (Dragon) |

Additional Attributes

格局 Structural Star	七殺 Seven Killings	偏印 Indirect Resource
用神 Useful God	Geng 庚 Metal	Ren 壬 Water
Conditions	Where both Geng Metal and Ren Water are revealed in the Heavenly Stems, this Day Master shall be blessed with success and nobility in life. In the absence of Geng Metal, however, Ren Water may be used to ensure that this Day Master is at least a knowledgeable, learned one.	
Positive Circumstances	Ren Water should preferably be revealed within the Heavenly Stems, in order to 'protect' Geng Metal. It would indeed be favourable to this Day Master, for Geng Metal to be at least available as a Useful God.	
Negative Circumstances	Strong Ding Fire directly countering Geng Metal.	

格局 Structural Star	食神 Eating God
用神 Useful God	Bing 丙 Fire
Conditions	Where two Bing Fire elements are seen in the Heavenly Stems, it would not benefit this Day Master –if Geng Metal is available as a Useful God. Under such circumstances, Ren Water or Gui Water must also be revealed.
Positive Circumstances	Ren Water and Gui Water, available as Useful Gods.
Negative Circumstances	Without Water, there would be no need for Bing Fire.

Day Master Jia 甲 Wood   **Month** Chen 辰 (Dragon)

Additional Attributes

格局 Structural Star	偏財 Indirect Wealth	正財 Direct Wealth
用神 Useful God	Wu 戊 Earth	Ji 己 Earth
Conditions	Where Earth (Resource Star) are in abundance and while Water Qi is entirely missing from the Earthly Branches, a Follow the Wealth Structure may be formed. Where the special structure is successfully formed, this person would enjoy an extraordinary life.	
Positive Circumstances	Geng Metal in the Heavenly Stems.	
Negative Circumstances	Earth should avoid meeting both Ren Water and Gui Water (which are this Day Master's Resource Stars).	

Dragon

格局 Structural Star	比肩 Friend	劫財 Rob Wealth
用神 Useful God	Jia 甲 Wood	Yi 乙 Wood
Conditions	Wood is strong and prosperous in a Chen (Dragon) Month. Where both Jia Wood and Yi Wood are also seen in the Heavenly Stems, female Day Masters may find their marriages short-lived. Meanwhile, male Day Masters will tend to be dominated by their wives.	
Positive Circumstances	Geng Metal in the Heavenly Stems.	
Negative Circumstances	Where Jia Wood and Yi Wood are revealed in the Heavenly Stems and Earthly Branches, this Day Master may possess a disreputable character.	

* Geng Metal is the primary Useful God for a Jia Wood Day Master born in a Chen (Dragon) Month; with Ren Water as its secondary Useful God.

Day Master   Jia 甲 Wood   **Month**   Chen 辰 (Dragon)

Summary

- Unless the Chen (Dragon), You (Rooster), Shen (Monkey), Xu (Dog) and Chou (Ox) Earthly Branches form a full Metal Structure, it would be unsuitable to employ Ding Fire as a Useful God for this Day Master.

- Ding Fire in the Earthly branches is acceptable.

- Geng Metal is necessary in order for this chart to excel.

Dragon

Jia 甲 Wood Day Master, Born in Fourth Month 四月

Si 巳 (Snake) Month
May 6th - June 5th

Do note that the dates provided above are subject to slight yearly variations. Please refer to the Ten Thousand Year Calendar for the accurate transition dates for each year.

| Day Master | Jia 甲 Wood | | Month | Si 巳 (Snake) |

日元 **Day Master**	月 **Month**

Jia
Yang Wood |

Si
Snake
Yin Fire |

For a Jia Wood Day Master born in a Si (Snake) Month, an Eating God Structure is formed where Bing Fire is revealed as one of the Heavenly Stems.

Where Geng Metal is revealed as one of the Heavenly Stems, a Seven Killings Structure is formed.

Where Wu Earth is revealed as one of the Heavenly Stems, an Indirect Wealth Structure is formed.

Should, however, neither Bing Fire nor Geng Metal nor Wu Earth happen to be revealed within the Heavenly Stems, one should select a Structure according to the BaZi Chart's most prominent Qi attribute at one's discretion.

Day Master Jia 甲 Wood

Month Si 巳 (Snake)

喜用神提要 **Regulating Useful God Reference Guide**

月 Month	用神 Useful God

4th Month 四月
Si 巳 (Snake) Month

癸
Gui
Yin Water

丁
Ding
Yin Fire

庚
Geng
Yang Metal

Snake

For a Si (Snake) Month, Gui Water, Ding Fire and Geng Metal are the Regulating Useful Gods.

As far as Regulating Useful Gods are concerned, Gui Water is this Day Master's primary choice for Useful God. This is because Gui Water provides 'moisture' to this Day Master.

Meanwhile, Geng Metal and Ding Fire serve as secondary Useful Gods to this Day Master.

Day Master Jia 甲 Wood

Month Si 巳 (Snake)

6th day of May – 5th day of June, Gregorian Calendar

Fire and Earth are strong in a (Si) Snake Month. Fire is considered 'blazing' and therefore producing 'hot' Earth.

This will inevitably cause this Day Master to become 'dry' and 'parched'. Hence, Water is critically needed to provide 'moisture' to this Day Master.

Given that Water is, however, 'trapped' and hence extremely weak in the month of Si (Snake) Month, Geng Metal is therefore needed as a supporting Useful God, in order to produce Water. In other words, Water is this Day Master's primary Useful God, with Metal as its secondary Useful God – as far as Regulating Useful Gods are concerned.

Of course, a Day Master born in an hour where Metal and Water happen to be strong enough can also use Wood as Useful Gods. Obviously if otherwise, there is the need for this Day Master to avoid encountering further Fire and Earth Qi as much as possible.

Day Master Jia 甲 Wood   **Month** Si 巳 (Snake)

Commentary

In addition to the preceding narratives on the potential Structures and scenarios resulting from a Jia Wood Day Master born in a Si (Snake) Month, the following circumstances also play their respective roles in determining the overall strength of this Day Master's BaZi Chart.

Note:

- Gui Water is the primary Regulating Useful God for this Day Master.

- Where possible, Geng Metal – as a secondary Useful God – should also be revealed; with Ding Fire present as well.

- Wu Earth and Ji Earth (Wealth Stars) should not penetrate to the Heavenly Stems.

- Wood is inevitably 'dry' and 'parched' in a Si (Snake) summer month. This is why Gui Water remains an indispensable Useful God to this Day Master.

- However, Water is 'trapped' and hence extremely weak this Month. But the Si (Snake) Earthly Branch contains Geng Metal as one of its Hidden Stems. Since Metal produces Water, any 'dryness' in this Day Master may be duly countered by having Geng Metal revealed in the Heavenly Stems.

- This is why Fire is only superficially strong this Month – it is weakened by the presence of Geng Metal (when revealed in the Stem) since it is rooted in the Si (Snake) Earthly Branch.

- Under the preceding circumstances, Fire Qi is hence gradually weakened. This is because Geng Metal produces Gui Water.

- As far as the ten Heavenly Stems are concerned, it is undesirable to have Jia Wood be seen without Geng Metal; just as Geng Metal should never be seen without Ding Fire.

- This is because Geng Metal is used to produce Water, which is an important Useful God to this Day Master. Where Geng Metal is used, however, there should be Ding Fire – at least in moderate quantity – to keep the former under control.

- This is why Gui Water, Geng Metal and Ding Fire are the most important Useful Gods to this Day Master.

- Nevertheless, there should still be a balance struck between the strength of Gui Water and Geng Metal Qi – since BaZi is all about the concept of Balance.

- While both are water, Gui Water is preferred to Ren Water.

- Where Ren Water (Indirect Resource Star) replaces Gui Water (Direct Resource Star) as this Day Master's primary Useful God, he or she shall be able to lead and enjoy a good quality of life. This Day Master would also be a learned, knowledgeable, magnanimous, benevolent and peace-loving person by nature. However, the achievement level would not be able to surpass the Gui Water Useful God.

- Although Bing Fire (Eating God Star) produces Earth (Wealth Star) - where Bing Fire, Wu Earth and Ji Earth are seen or encountered in the Heavenly Stems – this Day Master may only be able to enjoy limited success in life. Nevertheless, he or she may still be able to prosper, albeit only to a modest extent.

35

Day Master Jia 甲 Wood   **Month** Si 巳 (Snake)

Additional Attributes

格局 Structural Star	正印 Direct Resource	七殺 Seven Killings	傷官 Hurting Officer
用神 Useful God	Gui 癸 Water	Geng 庚 Metal	Ding 丁 Fire
Conditions	Where only Gui Water, Geng Metal and Ding Fire are revealed simultaneously in the Heavenly Stems, this Day Master shall be able to enjoy an extremely prosperous, happy and fulfilled life.		
Positive Circumstances	Fire is very strong in a Si (Snake) Month. This is why without Geng Metal as its source, the ability of Gui Water to serve as this Day Master's Useful God would still be extremely limited.		
Negative Circumstances	Where Bing Fire and Wu Earth are revealed in the Heavenly Stems, this Day Master may lack a sense of purpose and direction in life.		

*   *Gui Water, Geng Metal and Ding Fire are the preferred Useful Gods for a Jia Wood Day Master born in a Si (Snake) Month.*

Day Master Jia 甲 Wood   **Month** Si 巳 (Snake)

Summary

- Gui Water is the primary Useful God to this Day Master.

- Without Geng Metal (this Day Master's Seven Killings Star) to produce Gui Water, the water will not be strong enough to support the Day Master. However, a Seven Killings Structure formed by Geng Metal must be accompanied by both Ding Fire (Hurting Officer Star) to keep it under control.

Snake

Jia 甲 Wood Day Master, Born in Fifth Month 五月

Wu 午 (Horse) Month
June 6th - July 6th

Do note that the dates provided above are subject to slight yearly variations. Please refer to the Ten Thousand Year Calendar for the accurate transition dates for each year.

| Day Master | Jia 甲 Wood | | Month | Wu 午 (Horse) |

日元 Day Master	月 Month

Jia
Yang Wood

Wu
Horse
Yang Fire

For a Jia Wood Day Master born in a Wu (Horse) Month, a Hurting Officer Structure is formed where Ding Fire is revealed as one of the Heavenly Stems.

Where Ji Earth is revealed as one of the Heavenly Stems, a Direct Wealth Structure is formed.

Should, however, neither Ding Fire nor Ji Earth happen to be revealed within the Heavenly Stems, one should select a Structure according to the BaZi Chart's most prominent Qi attribute at one's discretion.

Day Master Jia 甲 Wood	**Month** Wu 午 (Horse)

喜用神提要 Regulating Useful God Reference Guide

月 **Month**	用神 **Useful God**

5th Month 五月
Wu 午 (Horse) Month

Gui
Yin Water

Ding
Yin Fire

Geng
Yang Metal

Horse

For a Wu (Horse) Month, Gui Water, Ding Fire and Geng Metal are the Regulating Useful Gods.

Wood is inevitably 'dry' and 'parched' this Month, due to the heat of summer.

This is why Gui Water is this Day Master's primary Useful God. In the absence of Gui Water, Ding Fire may be used as a secondary Useful God.

This Day Master would also fare favorably in life, when entering or undergoing a Water cycles.

Where Wood is overly strong, Geng Metal may be used to keep it under control. Likewise, should Geng Metal happen to be strong, Ding Fire may be used to keep it under control. Geng Metal without Ding Fire is useless metal.

| Day Master | Jia 甲 Wood | Month | Wu 午 (Horse) |

6th day of June – 6th day of July, Gregorian Calendar

Horse

Fire is extremely strong in a Wu (Horse) Month – and hence invariably clash with Metal and Water Qi, which are this Day Master's Useful Gods.

Jia Wood is at its weakest, this Month.

Where Metal and Water are present in abundance, however, they would be able to serve as Regulating – as well as Medicating – Useful Gods to an otherwise weak Day Master. Under such circumstances, Earth would also be 'moist' and 'wet' and therefore made productive. Where such circumstances are present, this chart is likely to belong to a powerful, wealthy and noble person.

Where Fire is present in abundance however, Wood should not be employed as a Useful God. This is to avoid having Wood produce and further strengthen Fire – which is already overly strong.

In any case, it is unfavorable if Earth should exert an overly strong control over Water. This is because where Earth – Wealth Star – is present in abundance; this Day Master would be severely weakened.

Water is therefore the primary Useful God to this Day Master, while Geng Metal serves as its secondary Useful God.

A Day Master born in an hour where Metal and Water happen to be strong may, however, choose Wood as its Useful God. Nevertheless, Fire and Earth Qi – of all the Five Elements – should be avoided the most.

Day Master Jia 甲 Wood **Month** Wu 午 (Horse)

Commentary

In addition to the preceding narratives on the potential Structures and scenarios resulting from a Jia Wood Day Master born in a Wu (Horse) Month, the following circumstances also play their respective roles in determining the overall strength of this Day Master's BaZi Chart.

Note:

Horse

- Where Gui Water is employed as a Useful God, it must be accompanied by Geng Metal as the secondary Useful God.

- Where Geng Metal is present in abundance or strength, Ding Fire must also be present to keep it under control.

- The formation of Wood and Fire Structures, where only Ding Fire is used – in the absence of Gui Water – would bring about extremely favorable outcomes to this Day Master. Indeed, this Day Master shall also possess a magnanimous, cultured and genteel personality. This is considered a special category of structures – known as Follow the Son.

- This Day Master's BaZi Chart would be of an excellent structure as well, where both Gui Water and Geng Metal are revealed in the Heavenly Stems.

Day Master Jia 甲 Wood　　　　**Month** Wu 午 (Horse)

Additional Attributes

格局 Structural Star	傷官 Hurting Officer
用神 Useful God	Ding 丁 Fire
Conditions	This Day Master would be 'trapped' or extremely weak, where Ding Fire forms a Hurting Officer Structure or while it enters a Fire Luck Period. Under such circumstances, serious unexpected setbacks may take place very often in this Day Master's life. His or her fortunes will only take a turn for the better, when entering the Wood or Water Luck cycles.
Positive Circumstances	Where Geng Metal (Seven Killings Star) is revealed in the Heavenly Stems, this Day Master would fare favourably in life, especially when entering a Water Luck Period.
Negative Circumstances	Where neither Ren Water nor Gui Water is revealed – even if this Day Master enters a Metal Luck Period – serious unexpected setbacks may still trouble this Day Master.

格局 Structural Star	正印 Direct Resource	七殺 Seven Killings
用神 Useful God	Gui 癸 Water	Geng 庚 Metal
Conditions	Where both Gui Water and Geng Metal are revealed, this person would enjoy a fabulous life. Filled with riches and good health.	
Positive Circumstances	Where Ren Water and Gui Water are revealed in the Heavenly Stems, this Day Master shall eventually prosper in life – although he or she may have to slog and toil at the early stages.	
Negative Circumstances	Where Geng Metal is present in abundance, this Day Master may lose all of his or her wealth; despite a relatively good start to life.	

Day Master Jia 甲 Wood　　　　**Month** Wu 午 (Horse)

Additional Attributes

五月 Fifth Month

Horse

格局 Structural Star	食神 Eating God	傷官 Hurting Officer
用神 Useful God	Bing 丙 Fire	Ding 丁 Fire
Conditions	Where Bing Fire and Ding Fire form a complete Fire Structure, Ding Fire (Hurting Officer Star) would be outshined. Although on the outlook the person enjoys respect and admiration, on the insider the person tends to feel discontented.	
Positive Circumstances	Where Water and Wood are encountered in moderate quantities, Earth (Wealth Star) may then be used to keep the balance between these elements.	
Negative Circumstances	Water is missing entirely from the chart. This person may suffer from poverty . He/she would most likelybe at a loss of sense of direction or purpose in life.	

格局 Structural Star	正財 Direct Wealth	偏財 Indirect Wealth
用神 Useful God	Ji 己 Earth	Wu 戊 Earth
Conditions	Wu Earth (Indirect Wealth Star) must be present; otherwise, it would be impossible for a Follow the Wealth Structure to be formed. Where the structure is successful formed, a life of greatness awaits. However, where the structure fails to be formed, this denotes a life that is dominated by financial problems and a overly dominating spouse.	
Positive Circumstances	The best-case scenario for this Day Master would be where Ren Water and Gui Water are also revealed in the Heavenly Stems.	
Negative Circumstances	Where neither Ren Water nor Gui Water (Resource Stars) are revealed in the Heavenly Stems, even the abundance of Earth (Wealth Star) may still result in this Day Master being afflicted by poverty in life.	

*　Gui Water is this Day Master's primary Useful God.
**　Ding Fire and Geng Metal are this Day Master's secondary Useful Gods.

Day Master Jia 甲 Wood   **Month** Wu 午 (Horse)

Summary

- Where a Fire Structure is formed, Ding Fire (Hurting Officer Star) may be outshined. And without Gui Water (Resource Star), this Day Master may not be able to enjoy an optimal quality of life.

Horse

Jia 甲 Wood Day Master, Born in Sixth Month 六月

Wei 未 (Goat) Month
July 7th - August 7th

Do note that the dates provided above are subject to slight yearly variations. Please refer to the Ten Thousand Year Calendar for the accurate transition dates for each year.

Day Master Jia 甲 Wood   **Month** Wei 未 (Goat)

日元 **Day Master**	月 **Month**

Jia
Yang Wood

Wei
Goat
Yin Earth

For a Jia Wood Day Master born in a Wei (Goat) Month, a Direct Wealth Structure is formed where Ji Earth is revealed as one of the Heavenly Stems.

Where Ding Fire is revealed as one of the Heavenly Stems, a Hurting Officer Structure is formed.

Where Yi Wood is revealed as one of the Heavenly Stems, an Goat Blade Structure may be formed when the conditions are completely met and supported by the Earthly branches.

Should, however, neither Ding Fire, Yi Wood nor Ji Earth happen to be revealed within the Heavenly Stems, one should select the BaZi Chart's most prominent Qi attribute at one's discretion.

Day Master Jia 甲 Wood   **Month** Wei 未 (Goat)

喜用神提要 **Regulating Useful God Reference Guide**

月 **Month**	用神 **Useful God**

6th Month 六月
Wei 未 **(Goat) Month**

癸
Gui
Yin Water

庚
Geng
Yang Metal

丁
Ding
Yin Fire

For a Wei (Goat) Month, Gui Water, Geng Metal and Ding Fire are the Regulating Useful Gods.

The primary Useful God in the first-half of the Month for this Day Master is usually the same as that of a Jia Wood born in Wu (Horse) Month; which is Gui Water.

Meanwhile, in the second-half of the Month, Geng Metal and Ding Fire are the most important Useful Gods.

49

| Day Master | Jia 甲 Wood | Month | Wei 未 (Goat) |

7th day of July – 7th day of August, Gregorian Calendar

Goat

The Wei (Goat) Earthly Branch also serves as storage for excess Wood Qi and also contains Ji Earth (Direct Wealth Star) as its main Hidden Stem.

Consequently, this Day Master would be weak or weakened; albeit not to an extreme extent. This is because the Ji Earth Hidden Stem in the Wei (Goat) Earthly Branch, once revealed in the Heavenly Stems, may combine with Jia Wood to form Earth in this month.

Meanwhile, Fire Qi is gradually diminishing in strength, at this time of the year.

Water, in small or moderate quantities, may hence be used to produce and strengthen Wood (this Day Master). If this is possible, this Day Master shall possess strong financial management abilities in life.

Similarly, Metal – also in small or moderate quantities – may equally be used to produce Water. And Water, in turn, serves as a Resource Star in producing and further strengthening this Jia Wood Day Master.

Day Master Jia 甲 Wood   **Month** Wei 未 (Goat)

Goat

Commentary

In addition to the preceding narratives on the potential Structures and scenarios resulting from a Jia Wood Day Master born in a Wei (Goat) Month, the following circumstances also play their respective roles in determining the overall strength of this Day Master's BaZi Chart.

Note:

- Gui Water, Geng Metal and Ding Fire are the preferred Useful Gods for this Jia Wood Day Master.

- It would not be necessary for Gui Water to be revealed in the Heavenly Stems, for it to serve as a Useful God.

- Where Ji Earth (Direct Wealth Star) is revealed in the Heavenly Stems, it should not be found side-by-side this Day Master, since Jia Wood and Ji Earth combine to form Earth.

- In order for a Follow the Wealth Structure to be formed, there must be Absence of Water Qi and an abundance of Earth Qi. When this structure is successfully formed, the person would live an extraordinary life.

- Consequently, without Water (a Resource Star), this Day Master may be afflicted by poverty in life. Indeed, he or she may also lack courage and character – while male Day Masters may be dominated by their wives. In other words, this Day Master may simply lack a sense of purpose or direction in life.

- Should a Wealth Structure be formed, and at the same time where the Heavenly Stems of the Month and Hour Pillars compete to combine with this Day Master (Ji Earth is found as the Heavenly Stems of the Month and Hour Pillars and compete with one another to combine with Jia Wood), male Day Masters may lead an aimless, wandering life. Meanwhile, female Day Masters may possess disreputable or 'loose' characters. Either way, the outcomes would be unfavorable.

- It is favourable to have Chen (Dragon) Earthly Branch present in the chart. With this the person is highly likely to enjoy prosperity and wealth in life.

- Conversely, without a Chen (Dragon) Earthly Branch present, this Day Master may only be able to lead an average life, at best.

Day Master	Jia 甲 Wood		Month	Wei 未 (Goat)

Additional Attributes

格局 Structural Star	傷官 Hurting Officer	七殺 Seven Killings
用神 Useful God	Ding 丁 Fire	Geng 庚 Metal
Conditions	Where one Ding Fire and one Geng Metal penetrate to the Heavenly Stems, this Day Master shall be blessed with fame and nobility in life. Where Ding Fire remains hidden while Geng Metal is revealed, this Day Master would only be an average or even mediocre one.	
Positive Circumstances	Geng Metal and Ding Fire penetrate to the Heavenly Stems	
Negative Circumstances	Absence of Ding Fire.	

Day Master Jia 甲 Wood　　　　　　**Month** Wei 未 (Goat)

Additional Attributes

Goat

格局 Structural Star	食神 Eating God	傷官 Hurting Officer	正財 Direct Wealth
用神 Useful God	Bing 丙 Fire	Ding 丁 Fire	Ji 己 Earth
Conditions	Where a complete Fire Structure is formed – leading to a Successful Follow the Son formation - this Day Master may enjoy extraordinary prosperity in life; although he or she shall may have to go through a few major hurdles in life. Where two Jia Wood and two Ji Earth Stems are seen, this Day Master shall prosper even more and become very wealthy in life.		
Positive Circumstances	Wood and Earth are found in their proper places in the BaZi Chart; while a Chen (Dragon) Earthly Branch and Gui Water (Direct Resource Star) are also present.		
Negative Circumstances	Where the Follow The Son structure is successfully formed, it is undesirable to enter Water luck. Where only ordinary structures are formed, Chen (Dragon) is needed. Where there is no Chen (Dragon) Earthly Branch or Gui Water as a Useful God present, this Day Master would only be an average, mediocre one.		

* Ding Fire and Geng Metal are the preferred Useful Gods for a Jia Wood Day Master born in a Wei (Goat) Month.

** There is a need for Gui Water as a Useful God in the form of Chen (Dragon).

Day Master Jia 甲 Wood   **Month** Wei 未 (Goat)

Summary

- Where Ji Earth is revealed in both the Heavenly Stems of the Month and Hour Pillars, both shall compete with one another to combine with this Day Master. Under such circumstances, however – regardless of whether it is a male or female Day Master – this Day Master shall suffer marriage related problems although there is certain amount of fame and achievement in his/her career life.

- Where a Follow the Wealth Structure is successfully formed, the person would, after much hardship finally be able to achieve an extraordinary financial status in life.

- For all other structures, without Water (Resource Star), any Structure formed would still be a substandard or inferior one.

Jia 甲 Wood Day Master, Born in Seventh Month 七月

Shen 申 (Monkey) Month
August 8th - September 7th

Do note that the dates provided above are subject to slight yearly variations. Please refer to the Ten Thousand Year Calendar for the accurate transition dates for each year.

| Day Master | Jia 甲 Wood | | Month | Shen 申 (Monkey) |

日元 Day Master	月 Month
 Jia **Yang Wood**	 *Shen* **Monkey** **Yang Metal**

For a Jia Wood Day Master born in a Shen (Monkey) Month, a Seven Killings Structure is formed where Geng Metal is revealed as one of the Heavenly Stems.

Where Wu Earth is revealed as one of the Heavenly Stems, an Indirect Wealth Structure is formed.

Where Ren Water is revealed as one of the Heavenly Stems, an Indirect Resource Structure is formed.

Should, however, neither Geng Metal nor Ren Water nor Wu Earth happen to be revealed amongst the Heavenly Stems, one should select a Structure according to the BaZi Chart's most prominent Qi attribute at one's discretion.

Day Master Jia 甲 Wood   **Month** Shen 申 (Monkey)

喜用神提要 **Regulating Useful God Reference Guide**

月 **Month**	用神 **Useful God**

7th Month 七月
Shen 申 (Monkey) Month

庚
Geng
Yang Metal

丁
Ding
Yin Fire

壬
Ren
Yang Water

Monkey

For a Shen (Monkey) Month, Geng Metal, Ding Fire and Ren Water are the Regulating Useful Gods.

Ren Water would be a suitable choice of Useful God to be employed; in the absence of Ding Fire. Ding Fire is the preferred choice as it helps controls the Seven Killings (Geng Metal) Qi.

| Day Master | Jia 甲 Wood | Month | Shen 申 (Monkey) |

8th day of August – 7th day of September, Gregorian Calendar

Geng Metal is extremely strong this month.

Where Metal and Water are simultaneously present in the chart, Wood shall invariably be 'wet' and also 'cold'.

As such, Fire is important in providing much-needed 'warmth' to this Day Master. Likewise, where Metal is present in abundance, more Wood – as a Companion Star – is required, in order to 'protect' and prevent this Day Master from becoming overly depleted.

Where Wood is cold, 'hot' or 'warm' Earth must be added, in order to control and prevent Water from 'overflowing'. Then and only then will be able to play its role as one of its Useful Gods.

Day Master	Jia 甲 Wood	Month	Shen 申 (Monkey)

Commentary

In addition to the preceding narratives on the potential Structures and scenarios resulting from a Jia Wood Day Master born in a Shen (Monkey) Month, the following circumstances also play their respective roles in determining the overall strength of this Day Master's BaZi Chart.

Note:

- It would be most favorable for this Day Master, where both Ding Fire and Geng Metal are revealed.

- Where this chart is using Ding Fire and Geng Metal, there is no need for Ren Water or Gui Water to be revealed in the Heavenly Stems.

- Geng Metal is at its strongest in a Shen (Monkey) Month. Nevertheless, it is only with the support of a controlled Geng Metal that this Day Master may remain well-balanced.

- Hence, where Geng Metal is employed as a Useful God, it must always be accompanied by Ding Fire.

- Should Geng Metal be revealed while Ding Fire is not, this Day Master may have to slog and toil in order to make his or her fortune in life.

- Where Ding Fire is revealed but Geng Metal remains hidden, this Day Master's achievements will be good, but not fantastic.

- Where three Geng Metal are seen but Ding Fire remains missing, this Day Master may be afflicted by physical disability, poor health and even loneliness in life.

59

| Day Master | Jia 甲 Wood | Month | Shen 申 (Monkey) |

Additional Attributes

格局 Structural Star	傷官 Hurting Officer	七殺 Seven Killings
用神 Useful God	Ding 丁 Fire	Geng 庚 Metal
Conditions	Where Geng Metal and Ding Fire are both revealed, this Day Master shall enjoy great succees in life.	
Positive Circumstances	It would also be extremely favourable for the Yin (Tiger), Mao (Rabbit) and Chen (Dragon) Earthly Branches to be present; otherwise, this Day Master may not be able to reap the full benefits from the presence of Ding Fire and Geng Metal as Useful Gods.	
Negative Circumstances	Where Geng Metal is revealed, without Ding Fire, this Day Master may have to slog and toil to make his or her fortune in life.	

Day Master Jia 甲 Wood   **Month** Shen 申 (Monkey)

Additional Attributes

格局 **Structural Star**	正財 Direct Wealth	偏財 Indirect Wealth
用神 **Useful God**	Ji 己 Earth	Wu 戊 Earth
Conditions	Geng Metal must also be present, where Wu Earth and Ji Earth (Wealth Stars) are present in abundance. Otherwise, Earth will counter Ren Water and Gui Water (Resource Stars), and this would not augur well in terms of financial prosperity for this Day Master.	
Positive Circumstances	Geng Metal and Ding Fire must be present as Useful Gods; otherwise, this Day Master would not be able to benefit from any favourable structure or circumstance present.	
Negative Circumstances	Where Ren Water or Gui Water (Resource Stars) is missing, this Day Master may find it difficult to make continious progress in life. Indeed, he or she may also be afflicted by poverty or constant cashflow problem.	

*   *Ding Fire and Geng Metal are the preferred Useful God for a Jia Wood Day Master born in a Shen (Monkey) Month.*

** *Where Ren Water or Gui Water (Resource Stars) is employed as a Useful God, it would be preferable not to Ji Earth penetrating to the Heavenly Stems.*

| Day Master | Jia 甲 Wood | | Month | Shen 申 (Monkey) |

Summary

- Without Ding Fire, it would be impossible for this Day Master's BaZi Chart to be of a good or favorable structure.

- Where a Resource (Water) Structure is formed, the Ding Fire Useful God would be countered. Under such circumstances, Ding Fire would be rendered useless. In this case it denotes a life of confliction – between success, relationship and health.

- Where two Ding Fire Heavenly Stems are seen – while there is neither a Hai (Pig) nor You (Rooster) Earthly Branch present – this Day Master shall find it very easy to achieve success in life due to help from many mentors.

- Where a Wealth Structure is formed and where the Earth is countering the Water. The person would find it hard to attain peach of mind.

- Ding Fire would control Metal better than Bing Fire.

Jia 甲 Wood Day Master, Born in Eighth Month 八月

You 酉 (Rooster) Month
September 8th - October 7th

Do note that the dates provided above are subject to slight yearly variations. Please refer to the Ten Thousand Year Calendar for the accurate transition dates for each year.

Day Master Jia 甲 Wood	**Month** You 酉 (Rooster)

日元 **Day Master**	月 **Month**
甲 *Jia* **Yang Wood**	酉 *You* **Rooster** **Yin Metal**

For a Jia Wood Day Master born in a You (Rooster) Month, a Direct Officer Structure is formed where Xin Metal is revealed as one of the Heavenly Stems.

Even if Xin Metal is not revealed as a Heavenly Stem, a Direct Officer Structure would still be considered to have been formed.

| Day Master | Jia 甲 Wood | | Month | You 酉 (Rooster) |

喜用神提要 **Regulating Useful God Reference Guide**

月 **Month**	用神 **Useful God**

8th Month 八月
You 酉 (Rooster) Month

Geng
Yang Metal

Ding
Yin Fire

Bing
Yang Fire

Rooster

For a You (Rooster) Month, Geng Metal, Ding Fire and Bing Fire are the Regulating Useful Gods.

Ding Fire is used to keep the Seven Killings where and if present under control.

Meanwhile, Bing Fire is treated as the preferred Regulating Useful God.

Day Master Jia 甲 Wood   **Month** You 酉 (Rooster)

8th day of September – 7th day of October, Gregorian Calendar

Metal is at its strongest in this month. With Xin Metal as a Direct Officer Qi being dominant this Month, Wood Qi would naturally be isolated or weak.

This is why additional Wood – Companion Star – is required to provide natural support to this Day Master. If this is possible, both this Day Master and Xin Metal would be strong and thriving. Under such circumstances, this Day Master shall be blessed with fame, financial success and happiness in life.

Water – in moderate quantities – is needed as a Regulating Useful God. This is especially true when Fire happens to be strong in the hour of birth. This can help prevent Jia Wood from being further countered and weakened.

Similarly, Fire and Earth will be advantageous in supporting this Day Master where Metal and Water Qi is dominant in the hour of birth. This would not only allow for Wood to be produced and strengthened; but also Metal to be duly kept under control. In other words, the presence of Fire and Earth would help negate and neutralize any ill-effects brought about by an abundance of Metal and Water.

Day Master Jia 甲 Wood

Month You 酉 (Rooster)

Rooster

Commentary

In addition to the preceding narratives on the potential Structures and scenarios resulting from a Jia Wood Day Master born in a You (Rooster) Month, the following circumstances also play their respective roles in determining the overall strength of this Day Master's BaZi Chart.

Note:

- Ding Fire and Bing Fire are this Day Master's important Regulating Useful Gods.

- Where a complete Metal Structure is formed - Ding Fire would serve as the main Regulating Useful God. In other cases, Bing Fire.

- It is undesirable for this Day Master to meet with Gui Water and Ren Water.

- Where the Earthly Branches form a complete Fire Structure, it would be easy for this Day Master to achieve success in life.

- Where both Geng Metal or Xin Metal is revealed in the Heavenly Stems – this Day Master may be afflicted by a mysterious illness towards middle-age.

- It is desirable to have Wu Earth and or Ji Earth (Wealth Stars) revealed in the Heavenly Stems along with the presence of Ding Fire.

- Where the Earthly Branches form a full Metal Structure, this Day Master may be susceptible to poor health and lingering illness in life.

- The same can also be said where Bing Fire and Ding Fire are in the Heavenly Stems without roots in the Branches - this Day Master may be afflicted by poor health and illness in the latter stages of his or her life.

- Where the Earthly Branches form a full Wood Structure – while Friend (Jia Wood) Stars are also revealed in the Heavenly Stems – only Geng Metal and Ding Fire are required as Useful Gods to this Day Master.

- The Regulating Useful Gods for a Jia Wood Day Master born in a Shen (Monkey) or You (Rooster) Month are basically similar.

| Day Master | Jia 甲 Wood | | Month | You 酉 (Rooster) |

Additional Attributes

格局 Structural Star	傷官 Hurting Officer	七殺 Seven Killings
用神 Useful God	Ding 丁 Fire	Geng 庚 Metal
Conditions	Where Ding Fire and Geng Metal are both revealed, this Day Master shall be blessed with success in life. Where Gui Water is also revealed, however, this Day Master may find success hard to come by, in life.	
Positive Circumstances	Geng Metal and Ding Fire rooted in the Earthly branches and penetrated to the Heavenly Stems.	
Negative Circumstances	Gui Water (a Direct Resource Star) is also revealed in the Heavenly Stems.	

格局 Structural Star	食神 Eating God	七殺 Seven Killings
用神 Useful God	Bing 丙 Fire	Geng 庚 Metal
Conditions	Where Bing Fire and Geng Metal are both revealed, this Day Master may be blessed with a modest level of wealth or prosperity in life.	
Positive Circumstances	Bing Fire in the Branches with Geng Metal in the Stems. Or vice versa.	
Negative Circumstances	Gui Water is also revealed in the Heavenly Stems.	

Day Master Jia 甲 Wood   **Month** You 酉 (Rooster)

Additional Attributes

Rooster

格局 **Structural Star**	食神 Eating God	傷官 Hurting Officer
用神 **Useful God**	Bing 丙 Fire	Ding 丁 Fire
Conditions	Where Bing Fire is revealed but Gui Water is missing, this Day Master can still achieve prosperity in life. Where the Earthly Branches form a full Fire Structure – with Earth also revealed – this Day Master shall also become very wealthy in life.	
Positive Circumstances	Wu Earth and Ji Earth (Wealth Stars) are also revealed.	
Negative Circumstances	Where Gui Water penetrates to the Heavenly Stems, this Day Master may be afflicted by poverty in life. This is because such a scenario would affect this Day Master's wealth luck, adversely.	

格局 **Structural Star**	七殺 Seven Killings	正官 Direct Officer
用神 **Useful God**	Geng 庚 Metal	Xin 辛 Metal
Conditions	Where the Earthly Branches form a full Metal Structure, this Day Master may be afflicted by poor health and illness in life. And where at the same time Bing Fire or Ding Fire is present, this Day Master may be susceptible to eye-related ailments in the latter stages of his or her life.	
Positive Circumstances	Bing Fire and Ding Fire are also revealed in the Heavenly Stems.	
Negative Circumstances	Without Fire, this Day Master may be inclined towards leading a solitary, hermit-like life.	

*   *Ding Fire and Bing Fire are this Day Master's preferred Useful Gods.*

** *Where only Jia Wood are revealed in the Heavenly Stems, Geng Metal would be this Day Master's primary Useful God.*

Day Master Jia 甲 Wood | **Month** You 酉 (Rooster)

Summary

- Gui Water (Direct Resource Star) should not be used or applied as a Useful God to this Day Master. This is because even Gui Water negates the important Fire Qi.

- Where Friend and Rob Wealth Stars are revealed in the Heavenly Stems, Geng Metal would be this Day Master's primary Useful God. Only with Geng Metal, will the Wood be useable.

Jia 甲 Wood Day Master, Born in Ninth Month 九月

Xu 戌 (Dog) Month
October 8th - November 6th

Do note that the dates provided above are subject to slight yearly variations. Please refer to the Ten Thousand Year Calendar for the accurate transition dates for each year.

| Day Master | Jia 甲 Wood | | Month | Xu 戌 (Dog) |

| 日元 **Day Master** | 月 **Month** |

甲
Jia
Yang Wood

戌
Xu
Dog
Yang Earth

For a Jia Wood Day Master born in a Xu (Dog) Month, an Indirect Wealth Structure is formed where Wu Earth is revealed as one of the Heavenly Stems.

Where Xin Metal is revealed as one of the Heavenly Stems, a Direct Officer Structure is formed.

Where Ding Fire is revealed as one of the Heavenly Stems, a Hurting Officer Structure is formed.

Should, however, neither Xin Metal nor Ding Fire nor Wu Earth happen to be revealed amongst the Heavenly Stems, one should select a Structure according to the BaZi Chart's most prominent Qi attribute at one's discretion.

Day Master Jia 甲 Wood   **Month** Xu 戌 (Dog)

喜用神提要 **Regulating Useful God Reference Guide**

Dog

月 **Month**	用神 **Useful God**
9th Month 九月 **Xu** 戌 **(Dog) Month**	庚 甲 丁 壬 癸 *Geng* *Jia* *Ding* *Ren* *Gui* **Yang** **Yang** **Yin** **Yang** **Yin** **Metal** **Wood** **Fire** **Water** **Water**

For a Xu (Dog) Month, Geng Metal, Jia Wood, Ding Fire, Ren Water and Gui Water are the Regulating Useful Gods.

Where Earth is in abundance, Jia Wood should be used to keep it under control.

Where Wood is in abundance, Geng Metal should be used to keep it under control.

In other situations, Ding Fire, Ren Water and Gui Water serve as auxiliary Useful Gods to this Day Master.

73

Day Master Jia 甲 **Wood**　　　**Month** Xu 戌 **(Dog)**

8th day of October – 6th day of November, Gregorian Calendar

Earth is invariably 'dry' in a Xu (Dog) late-autumn month. This is why Water is an indispensable – Useful God, in providing much-needed 'moisture' to this Day Master.

With Water Qi present, Jia Wood – which is dry would get the needed nourishment.

Wood is, however, not a preferred Useful God for this Day Master born – especially in an hour where Fire Qi happens to be strong and while Water is missing. This is because Wood produces and strengthens Fire.

Day Master   Jia 甲 Wood   **Month**   Xu 戌 **(Dog)**

Commentary

In addition to the preceding narratives on the potential Structures and scenarios resulting from a Jia Wood Day Master born in a Xu (Dog) Month, the following circumstances also play their respective roles in determining the overall strength of this Day Master's BaZi Chart.

Note:

- Earth is 'dry' in a Xu (Dog) Month.

- Much will depend on the presence or absence of Geng Metal – as a Useful God – for this Day Master. Geng Metal turns Wood in this season into a useful element.

- Where Geng Metal is used, however, it must always be accompanied by Ding Fire.

- In addition, Water must not be missing or lacking from the chart. This is because of the 'dry' state of Earth, this Month.

- Where Wu Earth and Ji Earth (Wealth Stars) are present in abundance and in strength in the absence of Water Qi, it would be possible for a Follow the Wealth Structure to be formed.

- It is undesirable for this Day Master to meet with Bing Fire. This is because Bing Fire has the capacity to wear off Geng Metal. Where found in the chart, this Day Master may lack sincerity and be inclined towards blaming others for failures in life.

- Where the Earthly Branches form a full Fire Structure, the Earth Qi becomes abundant naturally. Under such circumstances, even the presence of Geng Metal would be to no avail to this Day Master. Consequently, this Day Master may be afflicted by loneliness and poverty in life.

Dog

| Day Master | Jia 甲 Wood | Month | Xu 戌 (Dog) |

Additional Attributes

格局 Structural Star	偏財 Indirect Wealth	正財 Direct Wealth
用神 Useful God	Wu 戊 Earth	Ji 己 Earth
Conditions	It is extremley desirable to have Ren Water, Ding Fire and Gui Water are present, this Day Master's BaZi Chart. Where only Water (Resource Star) is available, this Day Master may still be blessed with wealth in life; albeit to only a modest extent.	
Positive Circumstances	Where Companion (Friend and Rob Wealth) Stars are revealed, Geng Metal would be this Day Master's primary Useful God. Without Geng Metal, this Day Master would only be an average, mediocre one.	
Negative Circumstances	Geng Metal is not seen in the Heavenly Stems, while Friend and Rob Wealth Stars are also not revealed.	

格局 Structural Star	七殺 Seven Killings
用神 Useful God	Geng 庚 Metal
Conditions	Ding Fire is this Day Master's primary Useful God. This star helps the Day Master control's the Seven Killings.
Positive Circumstances	Ding Fire penetrating to the Heavenly Stems.
Negative Circumstances	Gui Water next to Ding Fire.

Day Master Jia 甲 Wood   **Month** Xu 戌 (Dog)

Additional Attributes

格局 **Structural Star**	食神 Eating God	傷官 Hurting Officer
用神 **Useful God**	Bing 丙 Fire	Ding 丁 Fire
Conditions	Where Bing Fire is used but Ding Fire is not, the person usually posses an insincere personality.	
Positive Circumstances	Wu Earth and Ji Earth (Wealth Stars) are also present and strong.	
Negative Circumstances	Where neither Geng Metal nor Xin Metal penetrates to the Heavenly Stems, this Day Master may be afflicted by poverty and find it difficult to progress in life – more so where Companion (Friend and Rob Wealth Stars) are seen.	

*   *Where the Day Master is strong, it is desirable to have Ding Fire and Geng Metal as the Useful Gods.*

九
月

Ninth Month

Dog

77

Day Master Jia 甲 **Wood**   **Month** Xu 戌 **(Dog)**

Summary

- Where a Wealth Structure is formed – while Companion Stars are also seen in the Heavenly Stems – this Day Master would belong to an average person with mere mediocre achievements in life. It is especially true in the absence of Geng Metal.

- It would be preferable to have Ding Fire (Hurting Officer Star) produce Earth (Wealth Star), instead of Bing Fire (Eating God Star).

Dog

九
月

Ninth Month

78

Jia 甲 Wood Day Master, Born in Tenth Month 十月

Hai 亥 (Pig) Month
November 7th - December 6th

Do note that the dates provided above are subject to slight yearly variations. Please refer to the Ten Thousand Year Calendar for the accurate transition dates for each year.

| Day Master | Jia 甲 Wood | Month | Hai 亥 (Pig) |

日元 Day Master | 月 Month

Jia
Yang Wood

Hai
Pig
Yin Water

For a Jia Wood Day Master born in a Hai (Pig) Month, an Indirect Resource Structure is formed where Ren Water is revealed as one of the Heavenly Stems.

Even if Ren Water is not revealed as a Heavenly Stem, an Indirect Resource Structure would still be considered to have been formed.

Where Jia Wood is revealed as one of the Heavenly Stems, a Thriving Structure may be formed when the conditions are completely met and fully supported by the Earthly branches.

Day Master Jia 甲 Wood   **Month** Hai 亥 (Pig)

喜用神提要 **Regulating Useful God Reference Guide**

月 Month	用神 Useful God

10th Month 十月

Hai 亥 (Pig) Month

庚 *Geng* **Yang Metal**   丁 *Ding* **Yin Fire**   丙 *Bing* **Yang Fire**   戊 *Wu* **Yang Earth**

亥 Pig

For a Hai (Pig) Month, Geng Metal, Ding Fire, Bing Fire and Wu Earth are the Regulating Useful Gods.

Where Geng Metal is employed as a Useful God, Ding Fire should also be used to keep Geng Metal under control.

Bing Fire, meanwhile, serves purely as a Regulating Useful God to this Day Master. Where Water is strong and prosperous, Wu Earth may be used to keep it under control.

Day Master Jia 甲 Wood	**Month** Hai 亥 (Pig)

7th day of November – 6th day of December, Gregorian Calendar

Given the early winter timing of this Day Master's birth, the Qi would invariably tend to be very cold, with Wood freezing up as well.

As such, Fire is needed as an indispensable Useful God for this Day Master. This is because Fire provides 'warmth' and produces Earth, which is also one of this Day Master's Useful Gods. Without these two elements, the chart will not be considered good quality.

Jia Wood is 'rooted', this Month. Even so, without Earth (Wealth Star), however, this Day Master may be continuously plagued by uncertainty in life.

Fire and Earth are the best Medicating Useful Gods for this Day Master.

Fire is the primary Useful God for a Day Master born in an hour where Metal happens to be strong, since it helps produces Earth – another important Useful God.

This Day Master requires more 'hot' or 'warm' Earth, in order to control and prevent Water from 'overflowing'.

Day Master Jia 甲 Wood   **Month** Hai 亥 (Pig)

Commentary

In addition to the preceding narratives on the potential Structures and scenarios resulting from a Jia Wood Day Master born in a Hai (Pig) Month, the following circumstances also play their respective roles in determining the overall strength of this Day Master's BaZi Chart.

Note:

- Geng Metal is perhaps very important Useful God for this Jia Wood Day Master. Without Geng Metal, Jia Wood's potential is unrealized. But Geng Metal must always be accompanied by Ding Fire.

- Bing Fire is needed to provide 'warmth' to the chart, as a supporting Regulating Useful God.

- At least one Bing Fire element is required as a Useful God, to provide 'warmth' and thaw the inevitable chill that accompanies this time of the year.

- It would indeed be favorable to this Day Master, where Geng Metal and Ding Fire are both revealed in the Stems and rooted in the Branches.

- Where Geng Metal is revealed but Ding Fire remains hidden, this Day Master would just fall short of in achieving it's greatest potential in life.

- Where Ding Fire and Geng Metal are revealed, this Day Master shall be blessed with authority, fame, wealth and status in life.

- Without Geng Metal, though, this Day Master may be afflicted by poverty in life due to pessimism, lack of courage and determination.

- Similarly, without Ding Fire, this Day Master may still struggle to accumulate or amass wealth in life – no matter how skillful or talented he or she may be.

- In the absence of Ding Fire, however, Bing Fire may be used as a substitute Useful God. However, this only means the chart can exert only up to half of it's true talent.

- Xin Metal simply cannot be used to replace Geng Metal – should the latter happen to be missing.

- It would also be considered favorable to this Day Master, should Friend Stars also happen to be seen in the Heavenly Stems.

| **Day Master** Jia 甲 Wood | | **Month** Hai 亥 (Pig) | |

Additional Attributes

格局 **Structural Star**	傷官 Hurting Officer	七殺 Seven Killings	偏財 Indirect Wealth
用神 **Useful God**	Ding 丁 Fire	Geng 庚 Metal	Wu 戊 Earth
Conditions	Where one Ding Fire and one Geng Metal are revealed, this Day Master shall enjoy prosperity in life. Better still, where Geng Metal, Wu Earth and Ding Fire are all revealed, this Day Master shall become extremely wealthy in life. Where one Geng Metal and one Wu Earth are revealed, this Day Master shall be blessed with wealth and longevity.		
Positive Circumstances	Wu Earth (Indirect Wealth Star) must not be missing, if this Day Master is to be a wealthy, noble one is life.		
Negative Circumstances	Where Ren Water penetrates to the Heavenly Stems, Wu Earth (Indirect Wealth Star) must be used to keep Ren Water under control.		

十月 Tenth Month

亥 Pig

Day Master Jia 甲 Wood   **Month** Hai 亥 (Pig)

Additional Attributes

格局 **Structural Star**	七殺 Seven Killings	偏財 Indirect Wealth
用神 **Useful God**	Geng 庚 Metal	Wu 戊 Earth
Conditions	Where only Wu Earth is present – while Geng Metal (Seven Killings Star) does not penetrate to the Heavenly Stems – Companion (Friend and Rob Wealth) Stars should not penetrate to the Heavenly Stems, either. Otherwise, this Day Master would only be an average, mediocre one.	
Positive Circumstances	Geng Metal is also firmly 'rooted', in order to 'protect' Wu Earth (Indirect Wealth Star).	
Negative Circumstances	Friend and Rob Wealth Stars also penetrate to the Heavenly Stems.	

*   *Geng Metal, Ding Fire and Wu Earth are the preferred Useful Gods for a Jia Wood Day Master born in a Hai (Pig) Month.*

Pig

十月 Tenth Month

Day Master Jia 甲 **Wood** **Month** Hai 亥 **(Pig)**

Summary

- Wu Earth (Indirect Wealth Star) may be regarded as a 'universal' or mutual Useful God for Jia Wood Day Masters born in this month.

- Ji Earth, however, lacks the strength to keep Water (Resource Star) under control.

- It would also be pointless to employ Water (Resource Star) as a Useful God to a Jia Wood Day Master born in this month.

Jia 甲 Wood Day Master, Born in Eleventh Month 十一月

Zi 子 (Rat) Month
December 7th - January 5th

Do note that the dates provided above are subject to slight yearly variations. Please refer to the Ten Thousand Year Calendar for the accurate transition dates for each year.

Day Master	Jia 甲 Wood	Month	Zi 子 (Rat)

日元 Day Master	月 Month
甲	子
Jia	*Zi*
Yang Wood	**Rat**
	Yang Water

For a Jia Wood Day Master born in a Zi (Rat) Month, a Direct Resource Structure is formed where Gui Water is revealed as one of the Heavenly Stems.

Even if Gui Water is not revealed as a Heavenly Stem, a Direct Resource Structure would still be considered to have been formed.

Day Master Jia 甲 Wood   **Month** Zi 子 (Rat)

喜用神提要 **Regulating Useful God Reference Guide**

月 Month	用神 Useful God		
11th Month 十一月 Zi 子 **(Rat) Month**	丁 *Ding* **Yin Fire**	庚 *Geng* **Yang Metal**	丙 *Bing* **Yang Fire**

For a Zi (Rat) Month, Ding Fire, Geng Metal and Bing Fire are the Regulating Useful Gods.

Since Wood is inevitably 'freezing' this Month, Ding Fire is this Day Master's primary Useful God – while Geng Metal is its secondary Useful God.

Meanwhile, Bing Fire serves as a supporting Useful God. It would also be ideal to have the Si (Snake) and Yin (Tiger) Earthly Branches present, if this Day Master's BaZi Chart is to be of an excellent structure.

十一月 Eleventh Month

Rat

Day Master Jia 甲 Wood **Month** Zi 子 (Rat)

7th day of December – 5th day of January, Gregorian Calendar

Water is invariably cold, in a Zi (Rat) winter month. Consequently, Wood is extremely weak due to the cold.

Without any 'hot' or 'warm' Earth to control it, Water Qi will overflow. And an overabundance of Water would 'uproot' Wood and cause it to 'float', too.

As such, Earth – Wealth Star – is one of the most important Useful Gods for this Day Master as it serves to control the Water.

But it is only when Fire is also available to provide 'warmth' that this Day Master would the Earth become useable. Fire also 'warms' or 'heats up' Water and this would allow the it to nourish this Day Master.

There is also the need for this Day Master to avoid meeting abundant Metal Qi without Fire. This is because Metal produces Water and therefore contributes to the 'coldness' and 'chill' already prevalent at this time of the year. Metal also counters Wood, whilst weakening Earth (Wealth Star).

Day Master Jia 甲 Wood   **Month   Zi 子 (Rat)**

Commentary

In addition to the preceding narratives on the potential Structures and scenarios resulting from a Jia Wood Day Master born in a Zi (Rat) Month, the following circumstances also play their respective roles in determining the overall strength of this Day Master's BaZi Chart.

Note:

- Ding Fire is this Day Master's primary Useful God, while Geng Metal is its secondary Useful God.

- Meanwhile, Bing Fire serves as a supporting or auxiliary Useful God.

- This Day Master should also avoid encountering Gui Water, where possible.

- A Jia Wood Day Master born in a winter month such as this should always be accompanied by Metal and Fire. In other words, it is ideal to have Bing Fire, Ding Fire and Geng Metal present in a chart.

- It is obviously extremely 'cold' and 'dark' in the winter months of Zi (Rat).

- Under such circumstances, Gui Water should not be revealed in the Heavenly Stems; nor should Bing Fire, Ding Fire and Geng Metal be missing from the Four Pillars of Destiny.

- This Day Master's BaZi Chart would be of an excellent structure, where Geng Metal and Ding Fire are both revealed in the Heavenly Stems – while the Si (Snake) and Yin (Tiger) Earthly Branches are also present.

- Where the Earthly Branches forms a full Water Structure – while Ren Water is also revealed in the Heavenly Stems – this Day Master may be inclined towards leading a wandering, aimless life. Even though Wu Earth and Ji Earth may be present, it would still be hard for this Day Master to find stability or establish a firm foothold in life.

- In the absence of Bing Fire, two Ding Fire Stems may be used to substitute for this absence. Indeed, if this is possible, this Day Master would at least be able to lead a stable, peaceful life.

91

| Day Master | Jia 甲 Wood | | Month | Zi 子 (Rat) |

Additional Attributes

格局 Structural Star	傷官 Hurting Officer	七殺 Seven Killings
用神 Useful God	Ding 丁 Fire	Geng 庚 Metal
Conditions	Where Geng Metal and Ding Fire are both revealed, Ding Fire (Hurting Officer Star) would be able to keep Geng Metal (Seven Killings Star) under control. Without Geng Metal, Jia Wood is useless wood. As long as neither Ren Water nor Gui Water penetrates to the Heavenly Stems, this Day Master shall enjoy prosperity and wealth in life. Where Ren Water and Gui Water penetrate to the Heavenly Stems, however, Wu Earth must also be present to keep Water under control.	
Positive Circumstances	Where the Yin (Tiger) and Si (Snake) Earthly Branches are present, they should not be found side-by-side each other, in order to avoid a Punishment Relationship from taking place. Presence of Ding Fire in the Heavenly Stems, rooted in the Branches.	
Negative Circumstances	Where Ren Water and Gui Water penetrate to the Heavenly Stems – while Wu Earth is missing – this Day Master would only be an average, mediocre one.	

92

Day Master Jia 甲 Wood   **Month** Zi 子 (Rat)

Rat

格局 Structural Star	食神 Eating God	偏財 Indirect Wealth
用神 Useful God	Bing 丙 Fire	Wu 戊 Earth
Conditions	Where Bing Fire and Wu Earth are both revealed, Bing Fire (Eating God Star) would produce and warm-up Wu Earth (Indirect Wealth Star). Under such circumstances, this Day Master shall enjoy continious prosperity and wealth in life. Where Ren Water and Gui Water penetrate to the Heavenly Stems, however, Wu Earth must also be present, in order to control Water and provide support to this Day Master.	
Positive Circumstances	Presence of Wu Earth to control the Water.	
Negative Circumstances	Gui Water (Direct Resource Star) also penetrates to the Heavenly Stems.	

格局 Structural Star	偏印 Indirect Resource
用神 Useful God	Ren 壬 Water
Conditions	Where the Earthly Branches form a full Water Structure, the absence of Wu Earth and Ji Earth may lead to this Day Master being afflicted by poverty and or extreme selffish conduct in life.
Positive Circumstances	Wu Earth and Ji Earth (Wealth Stars) are also revealed in the Heavenly Stems.
Negative Circumstances	Absence of Earth Qi.

93

Day Master Jia 甲 Wood   **Month** Zi 子 (Rat)

格局 **Structural Star**	正印 Direct Resource
用神 **Useful God**	Gui 癸 Water
Conditions	Where the relevant Earthly Branches form a full Water Structure, this Day Master may be afflicted by poverty, if there is no Earth and Fire present to neutralize Water. Nevertheless, even the presence of Wu Earth and Ji Earth would be to no avail to this Day Master.
Positive Circumstances	Earth and Fire Qi
Negative Circumstances	Abundance of Water.

*   Geng Metal must always be accompanied by Ding Fire. In addition, it would also be ideal for the Yin (Tiger) and Si (Snake) Earthly Branches to be present.

** Where the Yin (Tiger) and Si (Snake) Earthly Branches are present, Bing Fire must be accompanied by Wu Earth.

Day Master Jia 甲 Wood   **Month** Zi 子 (Rat)

Summary

- Geng Metal, Ding Fire and Bing Fire are essential components for the quality of this Jia Wood.

Rat

Jia 甲 Wood Day Master, Born in Twelfth Month 十二月

Chou 丑 (Ox) Month
January 6th - February 3rd

Do note that the dates provided above are subject to slight yearly variations. Please refer to the Ten Thousand Year Calendar for the accurate transition dates for each year.

| Day Master | Jia 甲 Wood | Month | Chou 丑 (Ox) |

| 日元 Day Master | 月 Month |

Jia
Yang Wood

Chou
Ox
Yin Earth

For a Jia Wood Day Master born in a Chou (Ox) Month, a Direct Wealth Structure is formed where Ji Earth is revealed as one of the Heavenly Stems.

Where Gui Water is revealed as one of the Heavenly Stems, a Direct Resource Structure is formed.

Where Xin Metal is revealed as one of the Heavenly Stems, a Direct Officer Structure is formed.

Should, however, neither Ji Earth nor Gui Water nor Xin Metal happen to be revealed within the Heavenly Stems, one should select the BaZi Chart's most prominent Qi attribute at one's discretion.

Day Master Jia 甲 Wood   **Month** Chou 丑 (Ox)

喜用神提要 **Regulating Useful God Reference Guide**

月 **Month**	用神 **Useful God**

12th Month 十二月
Chou 丑 (Ox) Month

Ding
Yin Fire

Geng
Yang Metal

Bing
Yang Fire

For a Chou (Ox) Month, Ding Fire, Geng Metal and Bing Fire are the Regulating Useful Gods.

Ding Fire should not be lacking – or worst, missing – in this Day Master's BaZi Chart. It is ideal should Fire be 'rooted' within the Si (Snake) or Yin (Tiger) Earthly Branches, as well.

Additional Jia Wood serves as a supporting Useful God to this Day Master.

Meanwhile, Geng Metal is used to chop Jia Wood – to produce Ding Fire.

99

Day Master Jia 甲 Wood   **Month** Chou 丑 (Ox)

6th day of January – 3rd day of February, Gregorian Calendar

Metal, Water and Earth basically share the same priority in a Chou (Ox) Month.

Wood, however, is 'obstructed' this Month. Even the presence of Earth would do little to allow Wood to be firmly 'rooted' and duly strengthened. This is because the Earth contains Metal inside to cut the roots.

This is why more Wood is first needed as a Useful God, in providing support to this Day Master. Fire – in abundance – is then needed, if this Day Master is to be an scholarly, wealthy and authoritative one in life.

It is highly undesirable for this Day Master to go through Metal and Water Qi. Otherwise, he or she may be plagued by lingering problems in life – particularly those brought about by his or her wealth or work.

Day Master Jia 甲 Wood   **Month** Chou 丑 (Ox)

Commentary

In addition to the preceding narratives on the potential Structures and scenarios resulting from a Jia Wood Day Master born in a Chou (Ox) Month, the following circumstances also play their respective roles in determining the overall strength of this Day Master's BaZi Chart.

Note:

- Ding Fire is this Day Master's primary Useful God, while Geng Metal is its secondary Useful God.

- Meanwhile, Bing Fire serves as a supporting Useful God.

- This Day Master should also avoid meeting Gui Water.

- It is obviously extremely 'cold' and 'dark' in the winter month of Chou (Ox).

- Under such circumstances, Gui Water should not be revealed in the Heavenly Stems; nor should Bing Fire, Ding Fire and Geng Metal be missing from the chart.

- It would be and ideal setup where Geng Metal and Ding Fire are both revealed in the Heavenly Stems – while the Si (Snake) and Yin (Tiger) Earthly Branches are also present.

- Where the Earthly Branches forms a full Water Structure – while Ren Water is also revealed in the Heavenly Stems – this Day Master may be inclined towards leading a wandering, aimless life. Even though Wu Earth and Ji Earth may be present, it would still be hard for this Day Master to find stability or establish a firm foothold in life.

- Where Fire is available to provide 'warmth' to this Day Master. Without Fire Qi, this Jia Wood may have very little progress in life. Most of the time, he or she will hit and stay on plateaus in life.

101

Day Master Jia 甲 Wood   **Month** Chou 丑 (Ox)

Additional Attributes

格局 **Structural Star**	傷官 Hurting Officer	七殺 Seven Killings	食神 Eating God
用神 **Useful God**	Ding 丁 Fire	Geng 庚 Metal	Bing 丙 Fire
Conditions	Only Bing Fire (Eating God Star) and Ding Fire (Hurting Officer Star) may be used to support and nourish the cold Earth – and therefore allow it to form a good quality Wealth Structure with this Day Master. Where Geng Metal is revealed but Ding Fire remains hidden – this Day Master may be able to prosper in life; albeit only to a modest extent. Where Ding Fire is revealed but Geng Metal remains hidden, however, this Day Master shall prosper and become wealthy in life.		
Positive Circumstances	Where only Ding Fire is present – but Geng Metal is missing – the abundant presence of Companion (Friend and Rob Wealth) Stars is needed to account for this deficit. Ding Fire appearing on the Heavenly Stems while firmly rooted in the Branches.		
Negative Circumstances	Without Geng Metal, this Day Master may lack determination, courage and faith in life. In addition, he or she may also possess an overly thrifty personality. Without Ding Fire, this Day Master may possess a cowardly disposition. Where Ding Fire is used in tandem with Companion (Friend and Rob Wealth) Stars – while Gui Water is also revealed in the Heavenly Stems – this Day Master would only be an average, mediocre one.		

*   *Ding Fire and Bing Fire are the important Useful Gods for a Jia Wood Day Master born in a Chou (Ox) Month.*

** *Xin Metal simply cannot replace or substitute for Geng Metal, as far as Useful Gods are concerned.*

Day Master Jia 甲 Wood   **Month Chou 丑 (Ox)**

Summary

- Without Geng Metal as a Useful God, this Day Master may be particularly susceptible to poor health and illness in life.

- In the absence of Ding Fire, though, Bing Fire may be used instead.

- Where both Ren Water and Gui Water are revealed in the Heavenly Stems – or the Earthly Branches form a Full Water Structure – this Day Master may find it extremely difficult to achieve success in life.

- Where Xin Metal were to form a Direct Officer Structure this Day Master- it would only be a mediocre chart at best.

Yi (乙) Wood Day Master

Overview:

Yi 乙 Wood is Yin Wood. It hence represents more 'yielding' forms of flora, such as flowers, grass and other 'softer', more pliant plants.

And like its Jia Wood counterpart, Yi Wood is equally affected by the availability – or absence – of sunshine and moisture.

But Yi Wood is unique in the sense that where Jia Wood is also available to provide it with support and shelter – just like the way rambling plants attach and wound themselves to sturdier trees in nature – it would be further strengthened. In addition, the presence of Wealth and Officer Stars would also go a long way towards ensuring that Yi Wood Day Masters remain well-balanced and thriving.

True to their Yin nature, Yi Wood Day Masters tend to be more flexible and adaptable to changing circumstances, compared to their Jia Wood counterparts. They are also good motivators; although they can be just as fickle and show-offish, if the mood strikes them.

Yi 乙 Wood Day Master, Born in First Month 正月

Yin 寅 (Tiger) Month
February 4th – March 5th

Do note that the dates provided above are subject to slight yearly variations. Please refer to the Ten Thousand Year Calendar for the accurate transition dates for each year.

| **Day Master** Yi 乙 Wood | **Month** Yin 寅 (Tiger) |

| 日元 **Day Master** | 月 **Month** |

乙
Yi
Yin Wood

寅
Yin
Tiger
Yang Wood

For a Yi Wood Day Master born in a Yin (Tiger) Month, a Direct Wealth Structure is formed where Wu Earth is revealed as one of the Hidden Stems.

Where Jia Wood is revealed as one of the Heavenly Stems, Goat Blade Structure may be formed when the conditions are completely met and supported by the Earthly branches.

Where Bing Fire is revealed as one of the Hidden Stems, a Hurting Officer Structure is formed.

Where Wu Earth is revealed as one of the Heavenly Stems, an Direct Wealth Structure may be formed when the conditions are completely met and supported by the Earthly branches.

Should, however, neither Bing Fire nor Wu Earth happen to be revealed within the Hidden Stems, one should select the BaZi Chart's most prominent Qi attribute at one's discretion.

Day Master Yi 乙 Wood   **Month** Yin 寅 (Tiger)

喜用神提要 **Regulating Useful God Reference Guide**

月 **Month**	用神 **Useful God**

1st Month 正月
Yin 寅 (Tiger) Month

丙
Bing
Yang Fire

癸
Gui
Yin Water

For a Yin (Tiger) Month, Bing Fire and Gui Water are its Regulating Useful Gods.

Bing Fire provides 'warmth' and hence dispels the chill still prevalent during this Month.

Meanwhile, Gui Water – in moderate quantities – may be used to provide 'moisture' to this Day Master.

It is undesirable to see Bing Fire to be 'trapped' or unable to exert its Qi. This happens when Gui Water is right next to it.

Day Master Yi 乙 Wood   Month Yin 寅 (Tiger)

4th day of February – 5th day of March, Gregorian Calendar

A Yin (Tiger) Month contains the elements of Fire, Earth and Wood in its Hidden Stems. This is a favourable condition in general for Yi Wood.

Given the early spring timing of this Day Master's birth, the environment would still be rather chilly.

Hence, Bing Fire, as a Useful God, should be revealed and also penetrate to the Heavenly Stems – to warm the Wood and to produce the Earth, which is this Day Master's Wealth Star. If this is attainable, this Day Master would be a strong, prominent one; which would also be able to enjoy long lasting prosperity in life.

正月

First Month

寅
Tiger

110

Day Master	Yi 乙 Wood	Month	Yin 寅 (Tiger)

Commentary

In addition to the preceding narratives on the potential Structures and scenarios resulting from a Yi Wood Day Master born in a Yin (Tiger) Month, the following circumstances also play their respective roles in determining the overall strength of this Day Master's BaZi Chart.

寅
Tiger

Note:

- As far as Regulating Useful Gods are concerned, Bing Fire is this Day Master's primary Useful God, with Gui Water serving as its secondary Useful God.

- Ren Water and Wu Earth should not penetrate to the Heavenly Stems.

- Being Yin in nature, Yi Wood is akin to 'gentler', 'softer' forms of Wood, such as the grass or rambling plants. As such, Water must be present or available, in order for Yi Wood to thrive and grow.

- In addition, it would also be preferable to have Fire – in moderate amounts – to support the growth of Yi Wood. Otherwise, this Day Master may be at risk of becoming overly 'moist' or 'wet', and just like the grass or weaker plants, its body, roots and parts may metaphorically be in danger of being weakened.

- This is why neither Bing Fire nor Gui Water should be missing as Useful Gods to this Day Master.

- A Day Master lacking Gui Water but having Bing Fire as its Useful God would at least be able to succeed in his or her career-related pursuits.

- Where Gui Water is present but Bing Fire absent, this Day Master may be in danger of lacking drive and determination and hence, lacking the ability to grow and progress in life.

- Given the 'softer', 'gentler' nature of Yi Wood, without Bing Fire and Gui Water, it lacks the strength and capacity to control Earth, which is this Day Master's Wealth Star. It also lacks the strength and ability to withstand Metal (its Direct Officer and Seven Killings Stars) from exerting a strong control over it.

- Wealth and Officer Stars are indeed unsuitable choices to be employed as Useful Gods for this Day Master.

| Day Master | Yi 乙 Wood | | Month | Yin 寅 (Tiger) |

- Where Wu Earth and Ji Earth – as Wealth Stars – are revealed and penetrate to the Heavenly Stems, Gui Water would be the most suitable choice as a Regulating Useful God to this Day Master. This is because both Wu Earth and Ji Earth have the capacity to keep Gui Water under control. Otherwise, it would be preferable to avoid Wu Earth and Ji Earth, since both have the capacity to negate the benefits brought about by this Day Master's Regulating Useful Gods. It should be remembered that Yi Wood lacks the strength to keep either Wu Earth or Ji Earth under control on it's own.

- It would not be favorable or beneficial to this Day Master, where Bing Fire is not revealed in the Heavenly Stems – but Metal and Water are instead present in abundance. The chart would invariably be 'wet', and the wood would not be able to grow. Under such circumstances, this Day Master's ability to grow and progress in life may be rather limited.

- Where both Bing Fire (Hurting Officer Star) and Gui Water (Indirect Resource Star) are revealed, this Day Master shall enjoy a great quality life.

- Where Bing Fire is present in abundance but Gui Water completely absent, a 'dry' scenario may be easily pictured. Under such circumstances, however, this Day Master may prosper and become wealthy in life; although his or her tastes and lifestyle would still be relatively simple ones.

Day Master Yi 乙 Wood   **Month** Yin 寅 (Tiger)

Additional Attributes

格局 **Structural Star**	傷官 Hurting Officer	偏印 Indirect Resource
用神 **Useful God**	Bing 丙 Fire	Gui 癸 Water
Conditions	Where both Bing Fire and Gui Water are revealed in the Heavenly Stems, this Day Master shall be blessed with success and fame in life. However, where Bing Fire is revealed and forms a Hurting Officer Structure with this Day Master – but Gui Water (Indirect Resource Star) remains missing – this Day Master's wealth prospects in life may be affected.	
Positive Circumstances	Where the Earthly Branches of Yin (Tiger), Wu (Horse) and Xu (Dog) form a Fire Structure, Gui Water (Indirect Resource Star) should at least be present in keep Fire Qi under control.	
Negative Circumstances	Where Gui Water is revealed in the Heavenly Stems but Bing Fire is not, the wood will be too cold and would not be able to grow.	

正月 First Month

Tiger

113

| Day Master | Yi 乙 Wood | | Month | Yin 寅 (Tiger) |

Additional Attributes

格局 **Structural Star**	正財 Direct Wealth	偏財 Indirect Wealth
用神 **Useful God**	Wu 戊 Earth	Ji 己 Earth
Conditions	Should Wu Earth or Ji Earth is revelaed in the Heavenly Stems, it should be accompanied by Bing Fire as well. Where Gui Water (Indirect Resource Star) penetrates to the Heavenly Stems meets with Wu or Ji Earth, this Day Master may be likened to Wood growing on 'wet' Earth. The preceding scenario is unfavourable. The chart is substandard.	
Positive Circumstances	Presence of Bing Fire in the Heavenly Stems.	
Negative Circumstances	Where Gui Water is revealed in the Heavenly Stems, the overall structure of this Day Master's BaZi Chart would be a substandard one.	

* *Bing Fire and Gui Water are the preferred Useful Gods for a Yi Wood Day Master born in a Yin (Tiger) Month.*

Day Master Yi 乙 Wood   **Month** Yin 寅 (Tiger)

Summary

- As a Useful God, Gui Water provides 'moisture' to this Day Master.

- In order for Gui Water to be successfully revealed in the Heavenly Stems, Bing Fire should also be revealed – or the Earthly Branches of Yin (Tiger), Wu (Horse) and Xu (Dog) should also be present in order to form a Fire Structure. This would be the ideal scenario.

- Bing Fire and Gui Water should not appear side by side.

正
月

First Month

寅
Tiger

115

Yi 乙 Wood Day Master, Born in Second Month 二月

Mao 卯 (Rabbit) Month
March 6th – April 4th

Do note that the dates provided above are subject to slight yearly variations. Please refer to the Ten Thousand Year Calendar for the accurate transition dates for each year.

Day Master Yi 乙 Wood	**Month** Mao 卯 (Rabbit)

日元 **Day Master**	月 **Month**
 Yi **Yin Wood**	 *Mao* **Rabbit** **Yin Wood**

For a Yi Wood Day Master born in a Mao (Rabbit) Month, the Earthly Branch of Mao (Rabbit) is Yi Wood's 'Prosperous' position.

Where Yi Wood is revealed as one of the Heavenly Stems, a Thriving Structure is definitely formed.

Even where Yi Wood is not revealed as one of the Heavenly Stems, A Thriving Structure is assumed when the conditions are completely met and supported by the Earthly branches.

Day Master Yi 乙 Wood   **Month   Mao 卯 (Rabbit)**

喜用神提要 Regulating Useful God Reference Guide

月 Month   ### 用神 Useful God

2nd Month 二月
Mao 卯 (Rabbit) Month

Bing
Yang Fire

Gui
Yin Water

For a Mao (Rabbit) Month, Bing Fire and Gui Water are its Regulating Useful Gods.

Gui Water is used to provide Wood with 'moisture', while Bing Fire is used to keep both in check.

| Day Master | Yi 乙 Wood | Month | Mao 卯 (Rabbit) |

6ᵗʰ day of March – 4ᵗʰ day of April, Gregorian Calendar

For a Yi Wood Day Master born in a Mao (Rabbit) Month, the Earthly Branch of Mao (Rabbit) is also Yi Wood's 'Prosperous' position. In other words, Wood is firmly 'rooted'.

A Day Master born this month would have the strength, drive and determination to generate wealth and prosper in life.

Bing Fire and Gui Water being the Regulating Useful Gods. Earth is the most important Useful God. Where this Day Master is duly supported by Fire and Earth as its Useful Gods – his or her wealth luck is life will be extremely promising.

Day Master   Yi 乙 Wood   **Month**   Mao 卯 (Rabbit)

Commentary

In addition to the preceding narratives on the potential Structures and scenarios resulting from a Yi Wood Day Master born in a Mao (Rabbit) Month, the following circumstances also play their respective roles in determining the overall strength of this Day Master's BaZi Chart.

Note:

Rabbit

- Bing Fire and Gui Water are the main Regulating Useful Gods for this Day Master.

- Yi Wood is firmly 'rooted' in a Mao (Rabbit) Month. Its immense strength is indeed comparable to that of Jia Wood's. This is why Geng Metal must not be absent from this Day Master's BaZi Chart. However, Geng Metal should not penetrate to the Heavenly Stems.

- Where Bing Fire and Gui Water are not available, Ding Fire and Ren Water may not be good substitutes. This is because Ren Water and Ding Fire have the tendency to combine with one another to form Wood.

- Geng Metal and Yi Wood must never be found side-by-side; since both will combine to form Metal.

| **Day Master** Yi 乙 Wood | | **Month** Mao 卯 (Rabbit) |

Additional Attributes

格局 **Structural Star**	劫財 Rob Wealth	比肩 Friend
用神 **Useful God**	Jia 甲 Wood	Yi 乙 Wood
Conditions	Where the Hai (Pig), Mao (Rabbit) and Wei (Goat) form a full Wood Structure, only Wood, Water and Fire may be suitably employed as Useful Gods, in order to arrive at a best-case scenario for this Day Master. Where Gui Water is present but Bing Fire absent, this Day Master shall still be able to prosper in life. Where Bing Fire is missing but Gui Water present, however, this Day Master may not be able to enjoy a good quality of life.	
Positive Circumstances	Bing Fire and Gui Water present in the chart.	
Negative Circumstances	Where only Gui Water is present as a Useful God, this Day Master may only be able to lead an average life, at best.	

Day Master   Yi 乙 Wood   **Month   Mao 卯 (Rabbit)**

Additional Attributes

格局 **Structural Star**	正官 Direct Officer	七殺 Seven Killings
用神 **Useful God**	Geng 庚 Metal	Xin 辛 Metal
Conditions	Geng Metal is needed to keep the overly strong Yi Wood from become too strong. But it should not appear in the Heavenly Stems.	
Positive Circumstances	Presence of Ding Fire to keep Geng Metal under control.	
Negative Circumstances	Absence of Ding Fire.	

*   *Bing Fire and Gui Water are the preferred Useful Gods for a Yi Wood Day Master born in a Mao (Rabbit) Month.*

| Day Master | Yi 乙 Wood | Month | Mao 卯 (Rabbit) |

Summary

- Neither Bing Fire nor Gui Water should be missing from the BaZi Chart.

- Even if Gui Water is revealed in the Heavenly Stems, it should only be in moderate amounts, instead of in abundance.

- Ding Fire weakens this Day Master, and also produces Earth – which is this Day Master's Wealth Star. Nevertheless, it would still be extremely favorable to this Day Master, where Ding Fire is used to keep Geng Metal – a Direct Officer Star – under control.

Chen 辰 (Dragon) Month
April 5th - May 5th

Do note that the dates provided above are subject to slight yearly variations. Please refer to the Ten Thousand Year Calendar for the accurate transition dates for each year.

Day Master Yi 乙 Wood   **Month** Chen 辰 (Dragon)

日元 **Day Master**	月 **Month**

Yi
Yin Wood

Chen
Dragon
Yang Earth

For a Yi Wood Day Master born in a Chen (Dragon) Month, a Direct Wealth Structure is formed where Wu Earth is revealed as one of the Heavenly Stems.

Where Gui Water is revealed as one of the Heavenly Stems, an Indirect Resource Structure is formed.

Where Yi Wood is revealed as one of the Heavenly Stems, a Thriving Structure may be formed when the conditions are completely met and supported by the Earthly branches.

Should, however, neither Wu Earth, Yi Wood nor Gui Water happen to be revealed within the Heavenly Stems, one should select a Structure according to the BaZi Chart's most prominent Qi attribute at one's discretion.

Day Master Yi 乙 Wood   **Month   Chen 辰 (Dragon)**

喜用神提要 **Regulating Useful God Reference Guide**

月 Month   用神 Useful God

3rd Month 三月
Chen 辰 (Dragon) Month

癸
Gui
Yin Water

丙
Bing
Yang Fire

戊
Wu
Yang Earth

For a Chen (Dragon) Month, Gui Water, Bing Fire and Wu Earth are its most important Regulating Useful Gods.

Wu Earth also serves as an Arbitrating Useful God, where the Earthly Branches form a Water Structure.

Day Master Yi 乙 Wood　　　　**Month** Chen 辰 (Dragon)

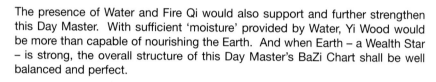

5th day of April – 5th day of May, Gregorian Calendar

The Chen (Dragon) Earthly Branch contains the Hidden Stems of Yi Wood, Wu Earth and Gui Water.

As such, Yi Wood – being firmly 'rooted' – is strong and prosperous. Under such circumstances, this Day Master would be a strong, thriving one and therefore also capable of achieving greatness in life.

The presence of Water and Fire Qi would also support and further strengthen this Day Master. With sufficient 'moisture' provided by Water, Yi Wood would be more than capable of nourishing the Earth. And when Earth – a Wealth Star – is strong, the overall structure of this Day Master's BaZi Chart shall be well balanced and perfect.

三月 Third Month

辰 Dragon

Day Master	Yi 乙 Wood	**Month**	Chen 辰 (Dragon)

Commentary

In addition to the preceding narratives on the potential Structures and scenarios resulting from a Yi Wood Day Master born in a Chen (Dragon) Month, the following circumstances also play their respective roles in determining the overall strength of this Day Master's BaZi Chart.

Note:

- Gui Water is the primary Useful God for a Yi Wood Day Master born in a Chen (Dragon) Month, while Bing Fire serves as its secondary Useful God.

- Where possible, this Day Master should also avoid encountering Ji Earth and Ren Water.

- Despite the gentler, softer nature of Yi Wood, Wood may nonetheless not be parted from Metal. Having said so, it would still be unsuitable for Geng Metal to be revealed in the Heavenly Stems.

- It is undesirable to have Ji Earth – Indirect Wealth Star – penetrate to the Heavenly Stems.

| Day Master | Yi 乙 Wood | | Month | Chen 辰 (Dragon) |

Additional Attributes

格局 **Structural Star**	傷官 Hurting Officer	偏印 Indirect Resource
用神 **Useful God**	Bing 丙 Fire	Gui 癸 Water
Conditions	Where both Bing Fire (Hurting Officer Star) and Gui Water (Indirect Resource Star) are present, this Day Master shall enjoy success in life. Where Bing Fire is available but Gui Water missing, however, this Day Master may experience mixed fortunes in life. Where Gui Water is present in abundance – and there is also a Si (Snake) Earthly Branch in the BaZi Chart – Wu Earth is needed to keep Water under control. Otherwise, this Day Master may be compelled to wander far and away in order to seek his or her fortunes in life.	
Positive Circumstances	Between Gui Water and Bing Fire, Gui Water is the preferred Useful God for this Day Master. Where Gui Water is present in abundance, Wu Earth must nonetheless penetrate to the Heavenly Stems, too.	
Negative Circumstances	Ji Earth and Geng Metal should not be revealed or penetrate to the Heavenly Stems. This is because both have the capacity to negate or 'destroy' the favourable stars in the BaZi Chart.	

格局 **Structural Star**	正官 Direct Officer
用神 **Useful God**	Geng 庚 Metal
Conditions	It is unfavourable to have Geng Metal next to Yi Wood Day Master.
Positive Circumstances	Only Ding Fire may be employed as a Useful God, in bringing about the best-case scenario for this Day Master.
Negative Circumstances	No Ding Fire penetrating to the Heavenly Stems.

Day Master Yi 乙 Wood   **Month   Chen 辰 (Dragon)**

Additional Attributes

格局 Structural Star	正印 Direct Resource	偏印 Indirect Resource	七殺 Seven Killings
用神 Useful God	Ren 壬 Water	Gui 癸 Water	Xin 辛 Metal
Conditions	Where the Earthly Branches form a Water Structure, this Day Master may be afflicted by poverty in life. Nevertheless, where Wu Earth (Direct Wealth Star) is seen, this person would still be a highly knowledgeable and enjoy moderate success in life. Where Xin Metal is encountered, Wu Earth is also needed to keep the Water produced by Xin Metal under control.		
Positive Circumstances	Wu Earth should be present in the BaZi Chart.		
Negative Circumstances	Wu Earth does not penetrate to the Heavenly Stems.		

*   *Gui Water and Bing Fire are the preferred Useful Gods for a Yi Wood Day Master born in a Chen (Dragon) Month. Where both Bing Fire and Gui Water are absent, this Day Master's BaZi Chart would be of an inferior or substandard structure.*

** *Ji Earth and Geng Metal should not penetrate to the Heavenly Stems, since both have the capacity to negate and 'destroy' the favourable elements.*

Day Master Yi 乙 **Wood**   **Month** Chen 辰 **(Dragon)**

Summary

- It would be difficult – to use Geng Metal on the Heavenly Stems as Yi and Geng has a tendency to combine.

- Where Ren Water and Gui Water are present in abundance, Wu Earth may be used to keep Water under control. Ji Earth would not suffice.

三
月
Third Month

辰
Dragon

Yi 乙 Wood Day Master, Born in Fourth Month 四月

Si 巳 (Snake) Month
May 6th - June 5th

Do note that the dates provided above are subject to slight yearly variations. Please refer to the Ten Thousand Year Calendar for the accurate transition dates for each year.

Day Master Yi 乙 Wood	Month Si 巳 (Snake)

日元 Day Master	月 Month

Yi
Yin Wood

Si
Snake
Yin Fire

For a Yi Wood Day Master born in a Si (Snake) Month, a Hurting Officer Structure is formed where Bing Fire is revealed as one of the Heavenly Stems.

Where Geng Metal is revealed as one of the Heavenly Stems, a Direct Officer Structure is formed.

Where Wu Earth is revealed as one of the Heavenly Stems, a Direct Wealth Structure is formed.

Should, however, neither Bing Fire nor Geng Metal nor Wu Earth happen to be revealed within the Heavenly Stems, one should select a Structure according to the BaZi Chart's most prominent Qi attribute at one's discretion.

Day Master   Yi 乙 Wood   **Month   Si 巳 (Snake)**

喜用神提要 **Regulating Useful God Reference Guide**

月 **Month**   用神 **Useful God**

4th Month 四月
Si 巳 (Snake) Month

Gui
Yin Water

For a Si (Snake) Month, Gui Water is the Regulating Useful God.

Since Bing Fire is particularly strong this Month, Gui Water serves the most important Regulating Useful God, in keeping Bing Fire under control.

Day Master Yi 乙 Wood　　　　**Month** Si 巳 (Snake)

6th day of May – 5th day of June, Gregorian Calendar

Snake

Fire is prosperous while Earth is strong in a (Si) Snake Month. As a result, Yi Wood may be weakened by such strong Fire.

This is why Water, in abundance, is needed as a Useful God, in order to produce and strengthen this Day Master accordingly. Similarly, the Geng Metal Hidden Stem found within the Si (Snake) Earthly Branch may also serve as a source to produce Water.

It is certain that Yi Wood shall invariably be 'wilted' and weak in a summer month.

As such, it would be highly unsuitable for Metal to be seen penetrating to the Heavenly Stems, especially in strength or abundance. Obviously, Metal counters Wood.

Water is indispensable, since it produces and serves as a Resource Star that strengthens Wood. In its presence, female Day Masters would enjoy good relationship luck – especially when it comes to finding (and keeping) a capable husband, as well as siring capable children.

Day Master   Yi 乙 Wood   **Month   Si 巳 (Snake)**

Commentary

In addition to the preceding narratives on the potential Structures and scenarios resulting from a Yi Wood Day Master born in a Si (Snake) Month, the following circumstances also play their respective roles in determining the overall strength of this Day Master's BaZi Chart.

Snake

Note:

- The Si (Snake) Earthly Branch contains Bing Fire, as its main Hidden Stems. This is why as far as Regulating Useful Gods are concerned; Gui Water remains indispensable, in order for this Day Master to survive.

- It is undesirable to have Wu Earth and Ji Earth penetrating to the Heavenly Stems. This is because Earth –is this Day Mastery's proverbial 'Achilles' Heel'. Earth directly counters the much needed Water.

- Fire is dominant in a Si (Snake) Month – and obviously, the overall environment would be hot. Yi Wood invariably 'withers' and becomes very weak, under such circumstances. This is why Gui Water remains the most important Useful God, in producing and strengthening this Day Master. In the absence of Gui Water, Ren Water may be used as a substitute Useful God.

- Without Water, this Day Master may be afflicted by poor health throughout life.

- Where Wu Earth and Ji Earth (Wealth Stars) – are present in abundance in the Heavenly Stems, there is a possibility that Wu Earth will combine Gui Water away. Under such circumstances, this Day Master may forsake or forgo his or her health, in pursuit of wealth and other material comforts.

- Where Gui Water is present in the Heavenly Stems, but not 'rooted' within the relevant Earthly Branches, it would however lack the strength required to function as a Useful God. Under such circumstances, Geng Metal would be needed, in order to produce Water.

- Where Gui Water is found in both the Heavenly Stems and Earthly Branches – with Geng Metal also present – this Day Master may ironically suffer from an 'overdose' of Useful Gods.

- Where Wu Earth and Ji Earth are found in abundance or revealed in the Heavenly Stems – while the Earthly Branches also form a full Fire Structure – this Day Master may serious lack wisdom, knowledge, inspiration and even a sense of opinion in life.

137

Day Master Yi 乙 Wood

Month Si 巳 (Snake)

- The formation of 'complete' Metal or Water Structures would, however, negate and counter the influence of Fire .

- Fire is obviously strong in a Si (Snake) Month. As such, it would be impossible for Geng Metal (Direct Officer Star) and Xin Metal (Seven Killings Star) to serve as prominent Useful Gods.

- Even if Gui Water happens to be revealed within the chart, the absence of Geng Metal penetrating to the Heavenly Stems would result in an average or mediocre Day Master – with corresponding results in life, regardless of the skills he or she may possess.

- Where Water is met, revealed or is formed as a structure, this Day Master may look forward to unexpected success or fortune in life.

Day Master Yi 乙 Wood   **Month** Si 巳 (Snake)

Additional Attributes

格局 **Structural Star**	偏印 Indirect Resource
用神 **Useful God**	Gui 癸 Water
Conditions	Without Geng Metal or Xin Metal to help produce Gui Water, this Day Master may only enjoy limited success or wealth in life. Where Geng Metal is available as a Useful God, it should not, however, combine with Yi Wood (to form Metal).
Positive Circumstances	The availability of Geng Metal and Xin Metal, to produce Gui Water. Gui Water must, however, be 'rooted'.
Negative Circumstances	Where Wu Earth is revealed in the Heavenly Stems – or the Earthly Branches form a Fire Structure – this Day Master may be afflicted by poverty as well as eye-related ailments in life.

* *Gui Water is the preferred Useful God for a Yi Wood Day Master born in a Si (Snake) Month.*

| Day Master | Yi 乙 Wood | Month | Si 巳 (Snake) |

Summary

- There is simply no substituting Gui Water (Indirect Resource Star) as Useful God to this Day Master.

- It would be to no avail to this Day Master, where the Earth Qi forms a Wealth Structure , should the chart have no Water Qi.

Yi 乙 Wood Day Master, Born in Fifth Month 五月

Wu 午 (Horse) Month
June 6th - July 6th

Do note that the dates provided above are subject to slight yearly variations. Please refer to the Ten Thousand Year Calendar for the accurate transition dates for each year.

| Day Master | Yi 乙 Wood | Month | Wu 午 (Horse) |

日元 Day Master	月 Month
Yi
Yin Wood |
Wu
Horse
Yang Fire |

For a Yi Wood Day Master born in a Wu (Horse) Month, an Eating God Structure is formed where Ding Fire is revealed as one of the Heavenly Stems.

Where Ji Earth is revealed as one of the Heavenly Stems, an Indirect Wealth Structure is formed.

Should, however, neither Ding Fire nor Ji Earth happen to be revealed within the Heavenly Stems, one should select a Structure according to the BaZi Chart's most prominent Qi attribute at one's discretion.

Day Master Yi 乙 **Wood**　　　　**Month** Wu 午 (Horse)

喜用神提要 Regulating Useful God Reference Guide

月 Month	用神 Useful God	

5th Month 五月
Wu 午 **(Horse) Month**

癸
Gui
Yin Water

丙
Bing
Yang Fire

For a Wu (Horse) Month, Gui Water and Bing Fire are the Regulating Useful Gods.

Priority should be accorded to Gui Water as the primary Useful God to this Day Master, in the first-half of the Month.

In the second-half of the Month, both Bing Fire and Gui Water should be used together.

五月 Fifth Month

Horse

Day Master Yi 乙 Wood   **Month** Wu 午 (Horse)

6th day of June – 6th day of July, Gregorian Calendar

Fire and Earth are prosperous in a Wu (Horse) Month, and would invariably clash with or counter Water.

As such, sufficient Water is needed to overcome the heat and dryness, as well as provide moisture to Earth and make it useable while at the same time strengthens Wood.

Thus, Metal – in moderate quantities – would be favorable since Metal serves as the source that produces Water.

Where Metal and Water are present, Wood may then be simultaneously used as yet another Useful God in strengthening this Day Master. This brings about a well-balanced scenario, since the presence of Metal and Water would also prevent Wood from producing too much Fire.

| Day Master | Yi 乙 Wood | | Month | Wu 午 (Horse) |

五月

Fifth Month

Horse

Commentary

In addition to the preceding narratives on the potential Structures and scenarios resulting from a Yi Wood Day Master born in a Wu (Horse) Month, the following circumstances also play their respective roles in determining the overall strength of this Day Master's BaZi Chart.

Note:

- Gui Water is the most important Useful God in a Wu (Horse) Month.

- Bing Fire also becomes an important Useful God in the second-half of this Month, followed by Gui Water. It is important that neither Gui Water nor Bing Fire be missing from the BaZi Chart.

- It is extremely favorable should Geng Metal happen to be the Heavenly Stem occupying the Year Pillar, with Gui Water the Heavenly Stem occupying the Hour Pillar.

- Where the pertinent Earthly Branches form a Fire Structure – while Gui Water is also revealed in abundance in the Heavenly Stems – this Day Master shall enjoy great success in his or her career-related pursuits.

- Where Gui Water is not revealed in the Heavenly Stems – but Fire and Earth are instead seen penetrating to and revealed within the Heavenly Stems – this Day Master may lack intelligence as well as a sense of purpose or direction in life.

Day Master Yi 乙 Wood   **Month** Wu 午 (Horse)

Additional Attributes

格局 **Structural Star**	傷官 Hurting Officer	食神 Eating God
用神 **Useful God**	Bing 丙 Fire	Ding 丁 Fire
Conditions	Where the Earthly Branches form a full Fire Structure, this Day Master would be a knowledgeable yet magnanimous one in life. It must be noted, however, that Gui Water must also be revealed in the Heavenly Stems, if this Day Master is to enjoy prosperity in life.	
Positive Circumstances	Gui Water is revealed in the Heavenly Stems. In the absence of Gui Water, Ren Water may be used – as a secondary choice.	
Negative Circumstances	Without Gui Water, this Day Master would only be able to lead an average life, at best. At worst, he or she may be afflicted by poor health in life.	

Day Master   Yi 乙 Wood   **Month   Wu 午 (Horse)**

Additional Attributes

格局 **Structural Star**	偏印 Indirect Resource
用神 **Useful God**	Gui 癸 Water
Conditions	Where Gui Water is employed as a Useful God, it must also be 'rooted' within the Earthly Branches. Otherwise, Geng Metal or Xin Metal would be needed as auxiliary Useful Gods, to produce Water.
Positive Circumstances	Gui Water, 'rooted' within the Earthly Branches.
Negative Circumstances	Gui Water is not 'rooted' within the Earthly Branches, while Wu Earth also penetrates to the Heavenly Stems.

147

| Day Master | Yi 乙 Wood | Month | Wu 午 (Horse) |

Summary

- In a Wu (Horse) - Fire Qi is dominant. Yi Wood is in danger of withering and becoming very weak. As such, without Gui Water, this Day Master's BaZi Chart would be of a substandard or inferior structure.

- Where possible, the Earthly Branches should not form a full Fire Structure.

- In the absence of Gui Water, Ren Water may be used as a Useful God instead.

Horse

Yi 乙 Wood Day Master, Born in Sixth Month 六月

Wei 未 (Goat) Month
July 7th - August 7th

Do note that the dates provided above are subject to slight yearly variations. Please refer to the Ten Thousand Year Calendar for the accurate transition dates for each year.

Day Master	Yi 乙 Wood	Month	Wei 未 (Goat)

日元 Day Master	月 Month
Yi Yin Wood	Wei Goat Yin Earth

For a Yi Wood Day Master born in a Wei (Goat) Month, an Indirect Wealth Structure is formed where Ji Earth is revealed as one of the Heavenly Stems.

Where Ding Fire is revealed as one of the Heavenly Stems, an Eating God Structure is formed.

Where Yi Wood is revealed as one of the Heavenly Stems, a Thriving Structure may be formed when the conditions are completely met and supported by the Earthly branches.

Should, however, neither Ding Fire, Yi Wood nor Ji Earth happen to be revealed within the Heavenly Stems, one should select the BaZi Chart's most prominent Qi attribute at one's discretion.

Day Master Yi 乙 Wood   **Month** Wei 未 (Goat)

喜用神提要 **Regulating Useful God Reference Guide**

月 **Month**	用神 **Useful God**

| **6th Month** 六月
Wei 未 (Goat) Month | 癸
Gui
Yin Water | 丙
Bing
Yang Fire |

Goat

For a Wei (Goat) Month, Gui Water and Bing Fire are the Regulating Useful Gods.

Gui Water is an indispensable Useful God, in providing moisture to both Earth and Wood. This makes it the primary Useful God to this Day Master.

Where Metal and Water Qi are present in abundance in the chart, however, Bing Fire assumes the role as the primary Useful God.

In a Wei (Goat) Month, Ren Water and Gui Water are important Useful Gods; although care should be taken not to have either of them 'contaminated' by Wu Earth or Ji Earth.

六月 Sixth Month

| Day Master | Yi 乙 Wood | Month | Wei 未 (Goat) |

7th day of July – 7th day of August, Gregorian Calendar

The Wei (Goat) Earthly Branch also serves as storage for excess Wood Qi. Thus, Yi Wood is firmly 'rooted' and hence strong in a Wei (Goat) Month.

Since Ji Earth is dominant this Month, it has the capacity to 'extract' from Ding Fire, to continue to produce Earth. Under such circumstances, both Earth (this Day Master's Wealth Star) and Yi Wood (this Day Master's Self Element) would be strong this month.

Water in moderate quantities would be needed in order to produce Wood – which may be dry, given prevailing circumstances. Without or with only little Water, this Day Master may only enjoy a limited level of financial success in life; although he or she would be capable of amassing wealth. For this Day Master to truly prosper in life, however, Metal in moderate quantities should be used to produce Water.

In any case, this Day Master would not encounter any difficulty getting help and support from Noble People (Gui Ren 貴人) in life.

Goat

Day Master Yi 乙 Wood   **Month** Wei 未 (Goat)

Commentary

In addition to the preceding narratives on the potential Structures and scenarios resulting from a Yi Wood Day Master born in a Wei (Goat) Month, the following circumstances also play their respective roles in determining the overall strength of this Day Master's BaZi Chart.

Goat

Note:

- Bing Fire and Gui Water are the preferred Useful Gods for this Yi Wood Day Master.

- Wu Earth and Ji Earth should neither be revealed nor penetrate to the Heavenly Stems.

- Should Wu Earth happens to be revealed in the Heavenly Stems, Jia Wood may be used to counter and keep it under control.

- Where Gui Water is not revealed in the Heavenly Stems – but Ren Water is, instead – this Day Master may only be able to lead an average life, at best.

- Where Wu Earth is revealed – but Jia Wood is also not seen penetrating to the Heavenly Stems – Water (this Day Master's Resource Star) is needed to help produce and strengthen Wood. Otherwise, this Day Master may only be able to lead an average life, at best.

- Where there are three Yi Wood Heavenly Stems present in the BaZi Chart, this Day Master may be afflicted by loneliness and pessimism in life.

- Where there are three Xin Metal Heavenly Stems present in the BaZi Chart, this Day Master may not only be afflicted by loneliness in life; he or she may also possess an arrogant personality.

- Where there are three Jia Wood Heavenly Stems present in the BaZi Chart, this Day Master may lead an aimless, wandering life. He or she may also possess a problematic attitude or personality. Under such circumstances, Bing Fire and Geng Metal are important Useful Gods required to negate any ill-effects brought about by such a BaZi Chart.

| **Day Master** Yi 乙 Wood | | **Month** Wei 未 (Goat) |

Additional Attributes

格局 **Structural Star**	正財 Direct Wealth	偏財 Indirect Wealth	劫財 Rob Wealth
用神 **Useful God**	Wu 戊 Earth	Ji 己 Earth	Jia 甲 Wood
Conditions	Where Wu Earth or Ji Earth are present, each shall counter Gui Water. This is why Jia Wood (Rob Wealth Star) is needed to 'protect' Gui Water.		
Positive Circumstances	Where Wu Earth, Ji Earth and Jia Wood are all present, this Day Master shall enjoy a great quality of life.		
Negative Circumstances	Without Jia Wood (Rob Wealth Star), this Day Master's BaZi Chart would be of a substandard or inferior structure.		

格局 **Structural Star**	七殺 Seven Killings
用神 **Useful God**	Xin 辛 Metal
Conditions	Where Bing Fire used together with Xin Metal, both should not be next to one another – since they combine to form Water. Otherwise, the success gained can be easily lossed or taken away by others.
Positive Circumstances	Both Bing Fire and Gui Water must be present as Useful Gods. Otherwise, this Day Master may be afflicted by poverty in life; as well as possess an arrogant character.
Negative Circumstances	Bing Fire and Xin metal side by side.

Day Master Yi 乙 Wood   **Month** Wei 未 (Goat)

Additional Attributes

格局 **Structural Star**	傷官 Hurting Officer	偏印 Indirect Resource
用神 **Useful God**	Bing 丙 Fire	Gui 癸 Water

Goat

Conditions	Without Bing Fire or Gui Water, this Day Master may find it extremely difficult to prosper in life.
Positive Circumstances	Where both Bing Fire and Gui Water is revealed in the Heavenly Stems – but Jia Wood (Rob Wealth Star) is present – This chart belongs to a an extremely capable leader. One bound to achieve great success in life.
Negative Circumstances	Where neither Bing Fire nor Gui Water is revealed but Jia Wood (Rob Wealth Star) is revealed, instead – this Day Master may lead an aimless, wandering life. In addition, he or she may also possess a problematic attitude or character.

*   *Where Geng Metal or Xin Metal are present, Bing Fire is this Day Master's primary Useful God.*

** *In all other cases, Gui Water would be this Day Master's primary Useful God.*

155

| Day Master | Yi 乙 Wood | Month | Wei 未 (Goat) |

Goat

Summary

- Geng Metal and Xin Metal should not be combined away. Where metal is present, then Jia Wood (Rob Wealth Star) must also be present and seen. Otherwise, this Day Master may find it difficult to prosper in life.

- Without Bing Fire and Gui Water are Useful Gods, this Day Master may experience negative Peach Blossom Luck – more so where Jia Wood (Rob Wealth Star) penetrates to the Heavenly Stems. Consequently, he or she may be inclined towards possessing a lascivious or sexually-immoral character.

Yi 乙 Wood Day Master, Born in Seventh Month 七月

Shen 申 (Monkey) Month
August 8th - September 7th

Do note that the dates provided above are subject to slight yearly variations. Please refer to the Ten Thousand Year Calendar for the accurate transition dates for each year.

Day Master	Yi 乙 Wood		Month	Shen 申 (Monkey)

日元 Day Master	月 Month

Yi
Yin Wood

Shen
Monkey
Yang Metal

For a Yi Wood Day Master born in a Shen (Monkey) Month, a Direct Officer Structure is formed where Geng Metal is revealed as one of the Heavenly Stems.

Where Wu Earth is revealed as one of the Heavenly Stems, a Direct Wealth Structure is formed.

Where Ren Water is revealed as one of the Heavenly Stems, a Direct Resource Structure is formed.

Should, however, neither Geng Metal nor Ren Water nor Wu Earth happen to be revealed amongst the Heavenly Stems, one should select a Structure according to the BaZi Chart's most prominent Qi attribute at one's discretion.

Day Master Yi 乙 Wood　　　　　**Month** Shen 申 (Monkey)

喜用神提要 **Regulating Useful God Reference Guide**

月 **Month**	用神 **Useful God**

7th Month 七月

Shen 申 (Monkey) Month

Bing
Yang Fire

Gui
Yin Water

Ji
Yin Earth

For a Shen (Monkey) Month, Bing Fire, Gui Water and Ji Earth are the Regulating Useful Gods.

Since Geng Metal is at its peak or strongest this Month, Bing Fire is used to keep it under control. Otherwise, Gui Water may also be used to weaken Geng Metal.

Regardless of whether Bing Fire or Gui Water is employed as a Useful God, Ji Earth nonetheless serves as this Day Master's 'intermediary' Useful God.

Day Master Yi 乙 **Wood**   **Month** Shen 申 **(Monkey)**

8th day of August – 7th day of September, Gregorian Calendar

Geng Metal Qi is dominant this month.

Yi Wood is particularly susceptible to being cut and countered by Geng Metal. In addition, there is also the risk that an overabundance of Water may drown out this Day Master.

Under these circumstances –Wood is in danger of being overly weakened. This is why Fire is the most important Useful God to this Day Master this month.

'Warm' Earth is required as a Useful God, in order to counter and prevent Water from 'overflowing'. This means both Fire and Earth Qi are needed simultaneously. If these elements are found, this Day Master can amass great wealth in life .

| Day Master | Yi 乙 Wood | Month | Shen 申 (Monkey) |

Commentary

In addition to the preceding narratives on the potential Structures and scenarios resulting from a Yi Wood Day Master born in a Shen (Monkey) Month, the following circumstances also play their respective roles in determining the overall strength of this Day Master's BaZi Chart.

Note:

- Bing Fire is the primary Useful God for this Yi Wood Day Master, with Gui Water as its secondary Useful God.

- Geng Metal is at its strongest in a Shen (Monkey) Month. As such, where Geng Metal combines with this Yi Wood Day Master, the latter would loose it's vitality.

- It is ideal to have Bing Fire, Gui Water and Ji Earth are all revealed in the Heavenly Stems.

- Neither Bing Fire nor Gui Water should be absent from the chart. If these two important stars are absent, the chart can only be mediorcre at best.

- Ji Earth is rarely treated as the main Useful God to this Day Master. This is because Ji Earth has the capacity to 'contaminate' both Ren Water and Gui Water.

- Where Ren Water and/or Gui Water are selected as Regulating Useful Gods, it is undesirable to have Ji Earth.

Day Master Yi 乙 Wood **Month** Shen 申 (Monkey)

Additional Attributes

格局 **Structural Star**	正官 Direct Officer
用神 **Useful God**	Geng 庚 Metal
Conditions	It would be difficult –for Geng Metal (Direct Officer Star) to serve as a Useful God to this Day Master. Ji Earth, Gui Water and Bing Fire must all be present, before Geng Metal can exert it's positive nfluence.
Positive Circumstances	Ji Earth penetrates to the Heavenly Stems.
Negative Circumstances	Ji Earth does not penetrate to the Heavenly Stems.

七月 Seventh Month

Monkey

162

Day Master Yi 乙 Wood   **Month** Shen 申 (Monkey)

Additional Attributes

格局 **Structural Star**	傷官 Hurting Officer	偏印 Indirect Resource
用神 **Useful God**	Bing 丙 Fire	Gui 癸 Water

Monkey

Conditions	Where Gui Water (Indirect Resource Star) is available but neither Ji Earth nor Bing Fire is, this Day Master may be compelled to be a 'jack of all trades', in order to make a living. Where Bing Fire (Hurting Officer Star) is present but Gui Water (Indirect Resource Star) does not penetrate to the Heavenly Stems, this Day Master may only be able to lead an average life, at best.
Positive Circumstances	Gui Water and Bing Fire present and penetrated to the Heavenly Stems.
Negative Circumstances	Where Gui Water is missing from the chart, this Day Master's BaZi Chart would be of a substandard or inferior structure.

*   *Ji Earth is the primary Useful God for a Yi Wood Day Master born in a Shen (Monkey) Month.*

**   *Bing Fire and Gui Water serve as supporting Useful Gods.*

| **Day Master** | Yi 乙 Wood | **Month** | Shen 申 (Monkey) |

Summary

- It should be noted that although Ji Earth is incapable of producing Metal, it has the capacity of burying and dirtying Metal as well.

- Where the presence of Metal results in a Follow the Killings Structure being formed, Water (this Day Master's Resource Stars) must be absent for the formation to be successful.

- Where Resource Stars are used, Earth should also be revealed amongst the Heavenly Stems. Without Earth, the Water (Resource) would be overbearing.

- Where Bing Fire, Gui Water and Ji Earth are completely missing from the BaZi Chart – this chart is inferior.

Yi 乙 Wood Day Master, Born in Eighth Month 八月

You 酉 (Rooster) Month
September 8th - October 7th

Do note that the dates provided above are subject to slight yearly variations. Please refer to the Ten Thousand Year Calendar for the accurate transition dates for each year.

| **Day Master** Yi 乙 Wood | **Month** You 酉 (Rooster) |

日元 **Day Master**	月 **Month**
 Yi **Yin Wood**	 *You* **Rooster** **Yin Metal**

For a Yi Wood Day Master born in a You (Rooster) Month, a Seven Killings Structure is formed where Xin Metal is revealed as one of the Heavenly Stems.

Even if Xin Metal is not revealed as a Heavenly Stem, a Seven Killings Structure would still be considered to have been formed.

Day Master Yi 乙 Wood **Month** You 酉 (Rooster)

喜用神提要 **Regulating Useful God Reference Guide**

月 **Month**	用神 **Useful God**

8th Month 八月
You 酉 (Rooster) Month

癸 *Gui* **Yin Water** 丙 *Bing* **Yang Fire** 丁 *Ding* **Yin Fire**

For a You (Rooster) Month, Gui Water, Bing Fire and Ding Fire are the Regulating Useful Gods.

Gui Water is this Day Master's primary Useful God in the first-half of the Month, with Bing Fire serving as its secondary Useful God.

In the second-half of the Month, however, Bing Fire serves as the primary Useful God, with Gui Water as the secondary Useful God.

In the absence of Gui Water, Ren Water may be used as a substitute Useful God in its stead.

Where the relevant Earthly Branches form a Metal Structure, though, Ding Fire is the preferred Useful God, in keeping Metal Qi under control.

167

Day Master Yi 乙 Wood   **Month** You 酉 (Rooster)

8th day of September – 7th day of October, Gregorian Calendar

Metal is at its strongest this month.

Furthermore, a Clash will take place, should the You (Rooster) and Mao (Rabbit) Earthly Branches happen to be found side-by-side in the BaZi Chart.

Under such circumstances, Wood will loose in the clash and become adversely affected, especially if there's no support from other elements.

This is why first and foremost, Friend Stars (Yi Wood) are needed to provide support to this Day Master. Next, Fire and Water – if available – may also be used to weaken and keep Metal, which is already strong, under control.

Water – in moderate quantities – is needed as a Regulating Useful God. This will indeed prevent Yi Wood from being further countered and weakened and nullifies the Metal – Wood clash.

八月

Eighth Month

酉 Rooster

| Day Master | Yi 乙 Wood | Month | You 酉 (Rooster) |

Commentary

In addition to the preceding narratives on the potential Structures and scenarios resulting from a Yi Wood Day Master born in a You (Rooster) Month, the following circumstances also play their respective roles in determining the overall strength of this Day Master's BaZi Chart.

Note:

- Bing Fire and Gui Water are equally important as Useful Gods to this Day Master.

- Where the Earthly Branches form a Metal Structure, Ding Fire must also be revealed in the Heavenly Stems (meaning rooted in the Earthly Branches as well), in order to keep Metal under control. Otherwise, this Day Master may be afflicted by poor health and illness in life.

- Where Metal and Water stars are simultaneously revealed in the Heavenly Stems, this Day Master would be a knowledgeable, learned one. Nevertheless, Xin Metal should not be revealed in the Heavenly Stems as well. (Note that the presence of Bing Fire and Gui Water is assumed.)

- Where Water and Fire is also revealed, this Day Master shall enjoy an excellent quality of life.

Day Master Yi 乙 Wood   **Month** You 酉 (Rooster)

Additional Attributes

格局 Structural Star	傷官 Hurting Officer	偏印 Indirect Resource
用神 Useful God	Bing 丙 Fire	Gui 癸 Water
Conditions	Where both Bing Fire (Hurting Officer Star) and Gui Water (Indirect Resource Star) are revealed in the Heavenly Stems, this Day Master shall be blessed with fame and prospertiy in life. Where possible, Bing Fire should preferably be revealed in the Heavenly Stem of the Hour Pillar.	
Positive Circumstances	Where Bing Fire is revealed but Gui Water is not, this Day Master may succeed – although his or her wealth would only be modest. Where Gui Water is revealed but Bing Fire is not, any fame this Day Master attains in life may not be sustainable or long-lasting.	
Negative Circumstances	With neither Bing Fire nor Gui Water present as Useful Gods, this Day Master's BaZi Chart would be of a substandard, inferior structure.	

格局 Structural Star	正官 Direct Officer	七殺 Seven Killings
用神 Useful God	Geng 庚 Metal	Xin 辛 Metal
Conditions	Where the Earthly Branches forms a full Metal structure, the absence of Gui Water and Ding Fire may cause this Day Master to be susceptible to poor health and illness in life. In the absence of Gui Water, Ren Water may be used instead.	
Positive Circumstances	Where Gui Water, Xin Metal and Ding Fire are all revealed, this Day Master shall enjoy extended prosperity in life.	
Negative Circumstances	Where Gui Water is revealed but Ding Fire is missing, this Day Master may not be blessed with longevity in life.	

Day Master Yi 乙 Wood   **Month** You 酉 (Rooster)

Additional Attributes

格局 **Structural Star**	正財 Direct Wealth	偏財 Indirect Wealth
用神 **Useful God**	Wu 戊 Earth	Ji 己 Earth
Conditions	Where Bing Fire, Gui Water and Wu Earth are all revealed, this Day Master may attain fame; albeit by taking an unconventional or radical approach in life.	
Positive Circumstances	Bing Fire, Gui Water and Wu Earth penetrated to the Heavenly Stems.	
Negative Circumstances	Jia Wood (Rob Wealth Star) penetrates to the Heavenly Stems.	

Rooster

| Day Master | Yi 乙 Wood | | Month | You 酉 (Rooster) |

Summary

- Without Ding Fire, this Day Master may be particularly susceptible to poor health and illness in life.

- Where Gui Water is revealed in the Heavenly Stems - Water may be used to weaken Metal, which is strong this Month. If this is possible, this Day Master shall excel in life.

八月

Eighth Month

Rooster

Yi 乙 Wood Day Master, Born in Ninth Month 九月

Xu 戌 (Dog) Month
October 8th - November 6th

*Do note that the dates provided above are subject to slight yearly
variations. Please refer to the Ten Thousand Year Calendar for the
accurate transition dates for each year.*

日元 Day Master	月 Month

Day Master Yi 乙 Wood

Month Xu 戌 (Dog)

Yi
Yin Wood

Xu
Dog
Yang Earth

For a Yi Wood Day Master born in a Xu (Dog) Month, a Direct Wealth Structure is formed where Wu Earth is revealed as one of the Heavenly Stems.

Where Xin Metal is revealed as one of the Heavenly Stems, a Seven Killings Structure is formed.

Where Ding Fire is revealed as one of the Heavenly Stems, an Eating God Structure is formed.

Should, however, neither Xin Metal nor Ding Fire nor Wu Earth happen to be revealed amongst the Heavenly Stems, one should select a Structure according to the BaZi Chart's most prominent Qi attribute at one's discretion.

Day Master Yi 乙 Wood   **Month** Xu 戌 (Dog)

喜用神提要 **Regulating Useful God Reference Guide**

月 Month	用神 Useful God

9th Month 九月
Xu 戌 (Dog) Month

Gui
Yin Water

Xin
Yin Metal

For a Xu (Dog) Month, Gui Water and Xin Metal are the Regulating Useful Gods.

Xin Metal serves as a resource for Water.

Where Yi Wood – encounters Jia Wood, the picture is akin to a rambler (Yi Wood) wrapping itself around a sturdy tree (Jia Wood), for protection and personal advantage.

| Day Master | Yi 乙 Wood | Month | Xu 戌 (Dog) |

8th day of October – 6th day of November, Gregorian Calendar

Earth is invariably 'leaden' and 'thick' in a Xu (Dog) month.

As such, this Day Master is in danger of becoming overly 'dry' or 'parched'. This is why Water is an indispensable Useful God, in providing much-needed 'moisture'.

Xu (Dog) Earthly Branch also contains Ding Fire, Xin Metal and Wu Earth as its Hidden Stems. Where water is present in the chart, this Day Master need not worry about its 'dry' condition.

Where Fire Qi happens to be strong – but Water Qi is missing – should not depend greatly on Wood, as a Useful God. This is because Earth, being strong and 'thick, would easily cause Wood to 'break'.

Day Master Yi 乙 Wood | **Month** Xu 戌 (Dog)

九
月

Ninth Month

Commentary

In addition to the preceding narratives on the potential Structures and scenarios resulting from a Yi Wood Day Master born in a Xu (Dog) Month, the following circumstances also play their respective roles in determining the overall strength of this Day Master's BaZi Chart.

Dog

Note:

- Gui Water is the primary Useful God for this Day Master; more so when Jia Wood or Xin Metal is also present or revealed in the Heavenly Stems.

- Would be ideal if this Yi Wood Day Master is 'rooted' in Yin (Tiger) Earthly or (Mao) Rabbit Branches.

- Where this Day Master meets Jia Wood – it can lend on the latter's strength to thrive. In life, the person would have the innate ability to recognize talent in others and able to garner help whenever help is needed.

- Where Gui Water is present but Xin Metal absent, this Day Master may only be able to lead an average life, at best. Where Ren Water, however, replaces Gui Water as a Useful God, the same outcomes apply – although this Day Master would be able to assume leadership or managerial responsibilities in life.

Day Master Yi 乙 Wood	**Month** Xu 戌 (Dog)

Additional Attributes

格局 **Structural Star**	偏印 Indirect Resource	七殺 Seven Killings
用神 **Useful God**	Gui 癸 Water	Xin 辛 Metal
Conditions	Where both Gui Water (Indirect Resource Star) and Xin Metal (Seven Killings Star) are revealed in the Heavenly Stems, this Day Master shall be blessed with success and fame in life.	
Positive Circumstances	Gui Water and Xin metal penetrating to the Heavenly Stems.	
Negative Circumstances	Where Gui Water is present but Xin Metal is missing, this Day Master may only be able to lead an average life, at best. Where Xin Metal is present but Gui Water is missing, this Day Master may be afflicted by poverty in life.	

格局 **Structural Star**	正印 Direct Resource	偏印 Indirect Resource
用神 **Useful God**	Ren 壬 Water	Gui 癸 Water
Conditions	Where the Earthly Branches forms a full Water formation, it is important that Wu Earth is also revealed in the Heavenly Stems.	
Positive Circumstances	Where Wu Earth penetrated to the Heavenly Stems	
Negative Circumstances	Absence of Wu Earth.	

Day Master Yi 乙 Wood   **Month** Xu 戌 (Dog)

Additional Attributes

格局 **Structural Star**	正財 Direct Wealth	偏財 Indirect Wealth
用神 **Useful God**	Wu 戊 Earth	Ji 己 Earth
Conditions	Where Earth is found in abundance amongst the Earthly Branches, it would be possible for a Follow the Wealth Structure to be formed. Nevertheless, there should not be any support from Water and Wood in order for this to happen.	
Positive Circumstances	Abundance of Earth Qi.	
Negative Circumstances	Avoid Friend, Rob Wealth and Resource Stars.	

* *Gui Water is the primary Useful God for a Yi Wood Day Master born in a Xu (Dog) Month.*

179

Dog

| Day Master | Yi 乙 Wood | Month | Xu 戌 (Dog) |

Summary

- Even if Gui Water is used to account for the absence of Xin Metal, it would still lack the strength that would be otherwise available, in the latter's presence. Without Xin Metal (Seven Killings Star) present, Water is considered fragile.

- Where the Earthly Branches of Chen (Dragon), Xu (Dog), Chou (Ox) and Wei (Goat) are all present, it would be possible for a Follow the Wealth Structure to be formed – with its corresponding benefits.

- For a Follow the Wealth Structure to be successfully formed – there must be an absence of Friend, Rob Wealth and Resource Stars.

Hai 亥 (Pig) Month
November 7th - December 6th

Do note that the dates provided above are subject to slight yearly variations. Please refer to the Ten Thousand Year Calendar for the accurate transition dates for each year.

| Day Master | Yi 乙 Wood | | Month | Hai 亥 (Pig) |

日元 **Day Master**	月 **Month**
 Yi **Yin Wood**	 *Hai* **Pig** **Yin Water**

For a Yi Wood Day Master born in a Hai (Pig) Month, a Direct Resource Structure is formed where Ren Water is revealed as one of the Heavenly Stems.

Even if Ren Water is not revealed as a Heavenly Stem, a Direct Resource Structure would still be considered to have been formed.

Where Jia Wood is revealed as one of the Heavenly Stems, a Goat Blade Structure may be formed when the conditions are completely met and fully supported by the Earthly branches.

Day Master Yi 乙 Wood   **Month** Hai 亥 (Pig)

喜用神提要 **Regulating Useful God Reference Guide**

月 **Month**	用神 **Useful God**
10th Month 十月 Hai 亥 (Pig) Month	丙 *Bing* **Yang Fire** 戊 *Wu* **Yang Earth**

For a Hai (Pig) Month, Bing Fire and Wu Earth are the Regulating Useful Gods.

Bing Fire is the primary Useful God for this Day Master.

Wu Earth is the second preferred Useful God in keeping Water under control.

Day Master	Yi 乙 Wood		Month	Hai 亥 (Pig)

7th day of November – 6th day of December, Gregorian Calendar

Water is dominant this month.

The Qi of the chart would invariably tend to be cold, with Wood 'moist' and 'wet'.

As such, Fire is needed as an indispensable Useful God for this Day Master. This is so that when it meets with Earth, this Day Master would be strong enough to control it – leading to a prosperous and wealthy.

Ren Water and Jia Wood are particularly strong in a Hai (Pig) Month. In other words, Wood Qi is firmly 'rooted' in its respective element.

An abundance of Fire Qi would, however, lead to an abundance of Earth, which is this Day Master's Wealth Star. Under such circumstances, the simultaneous presence of Metal and Water would allow this Day Master to become famous and noble in life.

Fire and Earth are the best Medicating Useful Gods for this Day Master. The absence of both elements may result in this Day Master struggling to find happiness and stability in life.

| Day Master | Yi 乙 Wood | | Month | Hai 亥 (Pig) |

十
月

Tenth Month

Pig

Commentary

In addition to the preceding narratives on the potential Structures and scenarios resulting from a Yi Wood Day Master born in a Hai (Pig) Month, the following circumstances also play their respective roles in determining the overall strength of this Day Master's BaZi Chart.

Note:

- Where Ren Water and Gui Water are revealed in the Heavenly Stems, rooted Wu Earth may be used to keep Water under control. This is because Wu Earth is one of this Day Master's Medicating and Regulating – Useful Gods.

- The Qi of Bing Fire is rapidly diminishing in a Hai (Pig) Month. As such, the purpose of Bing Fire – as a Useful God – is merely to provide 'warmth' to this Day Master, while it still can. Bing Fire is not meant to produce or counter away any of the other elements, which may support or weaken this Day Master.

- As such, there is a need to avoid having Ren Water and Gui Water in abundance. This is because both have the capacity to counter and hence weaken the ability of Bing Fire to provide 'warmth'.

- Where Water is present in abundance, Wu Earth may be used to keep Water under control.

- Water is already strong in a Hai (Pig) Month. And where Bing Fire and Wu Earth are also seen penetrating to the Heavenly Stems, this Day Master will be able to prosper and become wealthy in life – even if fame may elude him or her.

- Where the Earthly Branches forms a full Water Structure – while Wu Earth is completely missing from the Heavenly Stems – this Day Master may lead an aimless or even wandering life.

- Where Ji Earth is seen, this Day Master may only be able to lead an average life, at best.

- Where the Earthly Branches form a full Wood Structure – while Bing Fire and Wu Earth are missing from the Heavenly Stems – this Day Master may still succeed in life; although there is also the possibility of encountering a string of failures, towards the end of this Day Master's life. This is because Water eventually floats the wood.

- Wu Earth – rather than Ji Earth – should be selected as a Useful God to this Day Master.

| **Day Master** Yi 乙 Wood | **Month** Hai 亥 (Pig) |

Additional Attributes

格局 **Structural Star**	傷官 Hurting Officer	正財 Direct Wealth
用神 **Useful God**	Bing 丙 Fire	Wu 戊 Earth
Conditions	A best-case scenario for this Day Master is where Bing Fire and Wu Earth are both revealed in the Heavenly Stems.	
Positive Circumstances	Where there is no Bing Fire (Hurting Officer Star) to produce Wu Earth (Direct Wealth Star), this Day Master would have to enter a Fire Luck Period, to enjoy favourable outcomes in life.	
Negative Circumstances	Ren Water, revealed in the Heavenly Stems. Where Wu Earth (Direct Wealth Star) is also missing, this Day Master may lead a life of instability and insecurity.	

Day Master Yi 乙 Wood　　　　　**Month** Hai 亥 (Pig)

Additional Attributes

Pig

格局 Structural Star	正印 Direct Resource	偏印 Indirect Resource
用神 Useful God	Ren 壬 Water	Gui 癸 Water
Conditions	Where Water forms a full Resource Structure – while Wu Earth (Direct Wealth Star) is unavailable to keep Water under control – this Day Master may lead a life of idleness.	
Positive Circumstances	Wu Earth (Direct Wealth Star) is selected as this Day Master's Useful God. Nevertheless, Ji Earth would not be able to serve the same purpose.	
Negative Circumstances	Although the Hai (Pig), Zi (Rat) and Chou (Ox) Earthly Branches form a Water Structure, Wu Earth (Direct Wealth Star) is not rooted in these Earthly Branches.	

*　Bing Fire and Wu Earth are the preferred Useful Gods for a Yi Wood Day Master born in a Hai (Pig) Month.

Day Master Yi 乙 Wood	**Month** Hai 亥 (Pig)

Summary

- A best-case scenario for this Day Master is where Bing Fire (Hurting Officer Star) produces Earth (Wealth Star) with this Day Master.

- Where Ren Water and Gui Water – are revealed in the Heavenly Stems, Wu Earth (Direct Wealth Star) is needed to keep Water under control. Indeed, in a Hai (Pig) Month, the specialty or particular function of Wu Earth is to counter and keep Water in check.

- Where a Wealth Structure is formed – while Wu Earth is revealed but Bing Fire remains hidden – and Friend Stars occupy the Heavenly Stems of the Month and Hour Pillars, this Day Master may lack a serious sense of purpose or direction in life. The person will be selfish and stubborn.

- Where Ren Water or Gui Water full Water structure with this Day Master – while Bing Fire (Hurting Officer Star), Wu Earth (Direct Wealth Star) and Geng Metal (Direct Officer Star) do not penetrate to the Heavenly Stems – this Day Master, regardless of its gender, may be afflicted by poverty in life.

Yi 乙 Wood Day Master, Born in Eleventh Month 十一月

Zi 子 (Rat) Month
December 7th - January 5th

Do note that the dates provided above are subject to slight yearly variations. Please refer to the Ten Thousand Year Calendar for the accurate transition dates for each year.

Day Master Yi 乙 Wood   **Month** Zi 子 (Rat)

日元 **Day Master**	月 **Month**

乙
Yi
Yin Wood

子
Zi
Rat
Yang Water

For a Yi Wood Day Master born in a Zi (Rat) Month, an Indirect Resource Structure is formed where Gui Water is revealed as one of the Heavenly Stems.

Even if Gui Water is not revealed as a Heavenly Stem, an Indirect Resource Structure would still be considered to have been formed.

Day Master Yi 乙 Wood **Month** Zi 子 (Rat)

喜用神提要 **Regulating Useful God Reference Guide**

月 **Month**	用神 **Useful God**
11th Month 十一月 **Zi 子 (Rat) Month**	丙 *Bing* **Yang Fire**

For a Zi (Rat) Month, Bing Fire is the Regulating Useful God.

Bing Fire is used to provide 'warmth' to Wood, which is otherwise extremely cold in a winter month.

It is undesirable for this Day Master to meet additional Gui Water.

| Day Master | Yi 乙 Wood | Month | Zi 子 (Rat) |

7th day of December – 5th day of January, Gregorian Calendar

Water and Wood are invariably 'cold', in a Zi (Rat) winter month. As such, it would be impossible for both these elements to be 'thawed', without Fire.

In addition, the absence of dry Wood will also make it impossible for Fire to 'burn' and be produced.

Fire is important, since it allows Earth to be 'thicker' and 'hot'; which in turn, keeps Wood firmly rooted and prevents it from 'drifting' or being 'washed away'.

Thus - Wood, Fire and Earth are all important Useful Gods to this Day Master.

It is undesirable for this Day Master to meet additional Metal and Water Qi, since both elements would only make the overall environment even 'colder', and therefore weaken Fire in the process.

Day Master	Yi 乙 Wood		Month	Zi 子 (Rat)

Commentary

In addition to the preceding narratives on the potential Structures and scenarios resulting from a Yi Wood Day Master born in a Zi (Rat) Month, the following circumstances also play their respective roles in determining the overall strength of this Day Master's BaZi Chart.

Note:

- Bing Fire is the solitary Useful God for this Day Master.

- Gui Water must not penetrate to the Heavenly Stems.

- Wu Earth may be used to keep Gui Water at bay, as this Day Master's Medicating Useful God.

- Water is in it's prime in the Zi (Rat) Month. As such, Ren Water and Gui Water should not penetrate to the Heavenly Stems.

- This month, the Water is incapable of producing Wood due to the inevitably freezing climate.

- Where Bing Fire is not revealed in the Heavenly Stems, this Day Master may be plagued by a lack of opportunities in life. The person may be talented, but find no avenues for such talents.

- It would be extremely favorable to this Day Master, where Bing Fire is revealed in the Heavenly Stems and firmly rooted in the Earthly Branches – whilst neither Ren Water nor Gui Water is seen penetrating to the Heavenly Stems.

- Where the Earthly Branches form a full Water Structure – with Ren Water or Gui Water is revealed and penetrates to the Heavenly Stems – this Day Master may find it extremely difficult to achieve a high level of authority or status in life; even if Wu Earth also penetrates to the Heavenly Stems. The best achievement would only be slightly above average. If Wu Earth is missing, then life would be miserable and solitary.

- Where Bing Fire and Wu Earth are both revealed and penetrate to the Heavenly Stems, this Day Master shall be blessed with a sense of peace and security in life. Success comes in many folds.

- Ding Fire is insufficient to counter the chill of a Zi (Rat) winter month. Where Bing Fire is not revealed – but Ding Fire is instead revealed and penetrates to the Heavenly Stems this Day Master may have to settle for an average life; sans a high level of position or power.

- If Ding Fire is thrice seen in the Heavenly Stems – while Bing Fire is missing from the chart – this Day Master may possess a pretentious, insincere character.

- Where three Ding Fire Heavenly Stems are used to replace Bing Fire as a Useful God, Jia Wood, Geng Metal are needed. This is because Geng Metal, Jia Wood cannot produce Ding Fire.

- If this Day Master is to enjoy good career and wealth luck, though, Jia Wood must be present within the chart.

- Without Jia Wood, this Day Master would only be a knowledgeable, learned one, at best but no substantial achievements in life.

- Where the Earthly Branches form a full Water Structure – while Ren Water or Gui Water is revealed in the Heavenly Stems, with Wu Earth and Bing Fire remain missing – this Day Master may be afflicted by poverty and poor health in life.

Day Master Yi 乙 Wood		**Month** Zi 子 (Rat)

Additional Attributes

格局 **Structural Star**	食神 Eating God	
用神 **Useful God**	Ding 丁 Fire	
Conditions	Jia Wood must also be seen, where this chart is using Ding Fire. Otherwise, he or she may be afflicted by loneliness and illness in life.	
Positive Circumstances	Where Jia Wood penetrates to the Heavenly Stems, it serves as a support for Yi Wood to 'cling' to.	
Negative Circumstances	Without Jia Wood, this Day Master may possess an unscrupulous character. This is because Yi Wood lacks the support of Jia Wood, and due to its Yin nature, has the tendency to 'sway', figuratively speaking.	

格局 **Structural Star**	正印 Direct Resource	偏印 Indirect Resource
用神 **Useful God**	Ren 壬 Water	Gui 癸 Water
Conditions	Where Water is in abundance, Wu Earth (Direct Wealth Star) is its primary Useful God. Otherwise, this Day Master may be afflicted by loneliness, poverty and poor health in life.	
Positive Circumstances	Earth (Wealth Star) is available to keep Water (Resource Star) under control. In any case, Bing Fire must also be available, to keep the chart warm.	
Negative Circumstances	Absence of Wu Earth penetrating to the Heavenly Stems.	

Day Master Yi 乙 Wood   **Month** Zi 子 (Rat)

Additional Attributes

Rat

格局 Structural Star	傷官 Hurting Officer	偏財 Indirect Wealth
用神 Useful God	Bing 丙 Fire	Ji 己 Earth
Conditions	Where both Ji Earth and Bing Fire are revealed in the Heavenly Stems, this Day Master shall enjoy prosperity in life. In the absence of Ji Earth, however, the presence of at least one or two Bing Fire Heavenly Stems (without Gui Water penetrating to the Heavenly Stems) would suffice to allow this Day Master to attain success and fame in life.	
Positive Circumstances	Bing Fire rooted and penetrated.	
Negative Circumstances	Gui Water (Indirect Resource Star) penetrates to the Heavenly Stems.	

* *Bing Fire is the primary Useful God for a Yi Wood Day Master born this month.*

** *Gui Water should not be revealed in the Heavenly Stems.*

| Day Master | Yi 乙 Wood | Month | Zi 子 (Rat) |

Summary

- It is highly undesirable to have Gui Water penetrated to the Heavenly Stems. If this is seen, the person may be afflicted by loneliness as well as a lack of sense of direction in life.

- Bing Fire governs the quality of this chart. It must be present.

- The purpose of Ji Earth – if used – is merely to counter and keep Gui Water under control. But Wu Earth does a better job.

- Where Ding Fire (Eating God Star) is selected as a Useful God, this Day Master should be able to enjoy an above-average life, and even make his or her fortune in life. Nevertheless, there should not be an overabundance of Ding Fire present; otherwise, this Day Master may also possess an unscrupulous or dishonest character.

Yi 乙 Wood Day Master, Born in Twelfth Month 十二月

Chou 丑 (Ox) Month
January 6th - February 3rd

Do note that the dates provided above are subject to slight yearly variations. Please refer to the Ten Thousand Year Calendar for the accurate transition dates for each year.

| **Day Master** Yi 乙 Wood | **Month** Chou 丑 (Ox) |

日元 **Day Master**	月 **Month**
Yi **Yin Wood**	*Chou* **Ox** **Yin Earth**

For a Yi Wood Day Master born in a Chou (Ox) Month, an Indirect Wealth Structure is formed where Ji Earth is revealed as one of the Heavenly Stems.

Where Xin Metal is revealed as one of the Heavenly Stems, a Seven Killings Structure is formed.

Where Gui Water is revealed as one of the Heavenly Stems, an Indirect Resource Structure is formed.

Should, however, neither Ji Earth nor Gui Water nor Xin Metal happen to be revealed within the Heavenly Stems, one should select the BaZi Chart's most prominent Qi attribute at one's discretion.

Day Master Yi 乙 Wood **Month** Chou 丑 (Ox)

喜用神提要 **Regulating Useful God Reference Guide**

月 **Month**	用神 **Useful God**

12th Month 十二月
Chou 丑 (Ox) Month

丙
Bing
Yang Fire

For a Chou (Ox) Month, Bing Fire is the Regulating Useful God.

Although the spring (Wood season) is rapidly approaching, it is still very cold this month.

As such, Bing Fire is used to provide much-needed 'warmth' to this Day Master.

Day Master Yi 乙 Wood   Month Chou 丑 (Ox)

6th day of January – 3rd day of February, Gregorian Calendar

In a Chou (Ox) Month, 'wet' or 'moist' Earth will cause Wood to be 'trapped'.

It is difficult for Yi Wood to grow without the warmth of Fire. More Wood is required to 'loosen' Earth and keep Metal Qi under control in order for this Yi Wood Day Master to grow and thrive.

It is undesirable for Water to penetrate to the Heavenly Stems.

| Day Master | Yi 乙 Wood | Month | Chou 丑 (Ox) |

Commentary

In addition to the preceding narratives on the potential Structures and scenarios resulting from a Yi Wood Day Master born in a Chou (Ox) Month, the following circumstances also play their respective roles in determining the overall strength of this Day Master's BaZi Chart.

Note:

- Bing Fire is the Useful God to this Yi Wood Day Master.

- It is undesirable to have access Water. Especially for Gui Water to penetrate to the Heavenly Stems.

- To be effective, Bing Fire must also be revealed in the Heavenly Stems.

- Wu Earth is needed to prevent Gui Water from harming the Bing Fire. This is why Wu Earth should be used in tandem with Bing Fire.

- Where Wu Earth is revealed twice or thrice in the Heavenly Stems, though, this Day Master would ironically be 'over-supported' or 'pampered'. Under such circumstances, Jia Wood is needed to keep Wu Earth under control.

- If Bing Fire remains hidden within the Earthly Branches –it would be difficult for this Day Master to achieve success in life, though he or she may encounter many opportunities.

- Where Ji Earth is revealed in the Heavenly Stems – instead of Wu Earth – this Day Master may still enjoy a good quality of life; provided Jia Wood is not revealed as well.

- A Follow the Wealth Structure is formed, where Ji Earth is revealed in the Heavenly Stems and when the entire chart is filled with Earth and there is absence of Wood.

Day Master Yi 乙 Wood　　　　　　**Month** Chou 丑 (Ox)

Additional Attributes

格局 Structural Star	傷官 Hurting Officer
用神 Useful God	Bing 丙 Fire
Conditions	Where Bing Fire (Hurting Officer Star) is revealed – while Gui Water (Indirect Wealth Star) is not – this Day Master shall prosper in life.
Positive Circumstances	Bing Fire, revealed in the Heavenly Stems.
Negative Circumstances	Gui Water penetrates to the Heavenly Stems.

十二月 Twelfth Month

Ox

Day Master Yi 乙 Wood   **Month** Chou 丑 (Ox)

Additional Attributes

Ox

格局 **Structural Star**	正財 Direct Wealth
用神 **Useful God**	Wu 戊 Earth
Conditions	Where Wu Earth and Bing Fire are revealed in the Heavenly Stems, Jia Wood (Rob Wealth Star) is needed to 'protect' this Day Master.
Positive Circumstances	Wu Earth is not rooted in the Branches.
Negative Circumstances	Where Wu Earth is rooted or appears in abundance.

* *Bing Fire is the preferred Useful God for a Yi Wood Day Master born in a Chou (Ox) Month.*

** *Gui Water should not penetrate to the Heavenly Stems, since it will counter Bing Fire.*

203

| Day Master | Yi 乙 Wood | Month | Chou 丑 (Ox) |

Summary

- Without Bing Fire, this chart is at best, mediocre.

- For a successful formation of a Follow The Wealth structure, the must be an absence of Friends and Rob Wealth Stars.

- Wu Earth is needed to prevent Gui Water from harming the needed Bing Fire.

Ox

About Joey Yap

Joey Yap is the founder of the Mastery Academy of Chinese Metaphysics, a global organization devoted to the teaching of Feng Shui, BaZi, Mian Xiang and other Chinese Metaphysics subjects. He is also the Chief Consultant of Yap Global Consulting, an international consulting firm specialising in Feng Shui and Chinese Astrology services and audits.

Joey Yap is the bestselling author of over 30 books on Feng Shui, Chinese Astrology, Face Reading and Yi Jing, many of which have topped the Malaysian and Singaporean MPH bookstores' bestseller lists.

Thousands of students from all around the world have learnt and mastered Classical Feng Shui, Chinese Astrology, and other Chinese Metaphysics subjects through Joey's structured learning programs, books and online training. Joey Yap's courses are currently taught by over 30 instructors worldwide.

Every year Joey conducts his 'Feng Shui and Astrology' seminar to a crowd of more than 3500 people at the Kuala Lumpur Convention Center. He also takes this annual seminar on a world tour to Frankfurt, San Francisco, New York, Toronto, London, Sydney and Singapore.

In addition to being a regular guest on various radio and TV shows, Joey has also written columns for The New Straits Times and The Star - Malaysia's two leading newspapers. He has also been featured in many popular global publications and networks like Time International, Forbes International, the International Herald Tribune and Bloomberg.

He has also hosted his own TV series, 'Discover Feng Shui with Joey Yap', on 8TV, a local Malaysian network in 2005; and 'Walking The Dragons with Joey Yap' on Astro Wah Lai Toi, Malaysia's cable network in 2008.

Joey Yap has worked with HSBC, Bloomberg, Microsoft, Samsung, IBM, HP, Alliance, GreatEastern, Citibank, Standard Chartered, OCBC, SIME UEP, MahSing, AutoBavaria, Volvo, AXA, Singtel, ABN Amro, CIMB, Hong-Leong, Manulife and others.

Author's personal websites :www.joeyyap.com

Follow Joey's regular updates on Twitter:

     www.twitter.com/joeyyap

Get to know Joey on Facebook:

     www.facebook.com/JoeyYapFB

EDUCATION
The Mastery Academy of Chinese Metaphysics:
the first choice for practitioners and aspiring students of the art and science of Chinese Classical Feng Shui and Astrology.

For thousands of years, Eastern knowledge has been passed from one generation to another through the system of discipleship. A venerated master would accept suitable individuals at a young age as his disciples, and informally through the years, pass on his knowledge and skills to them. His disciples in turn, would take on their own disciples, as a means to perpetuate knowledge or skills.

This system served the purpose of restricting the transfer of knowledge to only worthy honourable individuals and ensuring that outsiders or Westerners would not have access to thousands of years of Eastern knowledge, learning and research.

However, the disciple system has also resulted in Chinese Metaphysics and Classical Studies lacking systematic teaching methods. Knowledge garnered over the years has not been accumulated in a concise, systematic manner, but scattered amongst practitioners, each practicing his/her knowledge, art and science, in isolation.

The disciple system, out of place in today's modern world, endangers the advancement of these classical fields that continue to have great relevance and application today.

At the Mastery Academy of Chinese Metaphysics, our Mission is to bring Eastern Classical knowledge in the fields of metaphysics, Feng Shui and Astrology sciences and the arts to the world. These Classical teachings and knowledge, previously shrouded in secrecy and passed on only through the discipleship system, are adapted into structured learning, which can easily be understood, learnt and mastered. Through modern learning methods, these renowned ancient arts, sciences and practices can be perpetuated while facilitating more extensive application and understanding of these classical subjects.

The Mastery Academy espouses an educational philosophy that draws from the best of the East and West. It is the world's premier educational institution for the study of Chinese Metaphysics Studies offering a wide range and variety of courses, ensuring that students have the opportunity to pursue their preferred field of study and enabling existing practitioners and professionals to gain cross-disciplinary knowledge that complements their current field of practice.

Courses at the Mastery Academy have been carefully designed to ensure a comprehensive yet compact syllabus. The modular nature of the courses enables students to immediately begin to put their knowledge into practice while pursuing continued study of their field and complementary fields. Students thus have the benefit of developing and gaining practical experience in tandem with the expansion and advancement of their theoretical knowledge.

Students can also choose from a variety of study options, from a distance learning program, the Homestudy Series, that enables study at one's own pace or intensive foundation courses and compact lecture-based courses, held in various cities around the world by Joey Yap or our licensed instructors. The Mastery Academy's faculty and make-up is international in nature, thus ensuring that prospective students can attend courses at destinations nearest to their country of origin or with a licensed Mastery Academy instructor in their home country.

The Mastery Academy provides 24x7 support to students through its Online Community, with a variety of tools, documents, forums and e-learning materials to help students stay at the forefront of research in their fields and gain invaluable assistance from peers and mentoring from their instructors.

MASTERY ACADEMY
OF CHINESE METAPHYSICS

www.masteryacademy.com

MALAYSIA
19-3, The Boulevard
Mid Valley City
59200 Kuala Lumpur, Malaysia
Tel : +603-2284 8080
Fax : +603-2284 1218
Email : info@masteryacademy.com

Australia, Austria, Canada, China, Croatia, Cyprus, Czech Republic, Denmark, France, Germany, Greece, Hungary, India, Italy, Kazakhstan, Malaysia, Netherlands (Holland), New Zealand, Philippines, Poland, Russian Federation, Singapore, Slovenia, South Africa, Switzerland, Turkey, U.S.A., Ukraine, United Kingdom

Introducing...
The Mastery Academy's E-Learning Center!

The Mastery Academy's goal has always been to share authentic knowledge of Chinese Metaphysics with the whole world.

Nevertheless, we do recognize that distance, time, and hotel and traveling costs – amongst many other factors – could actually hinder people from enrolling for a classroom-based course. But with the advent and amazing advance of IT today, NOT any more!

With this in mind, we have invested heavily in IT, to conceive what is probably the first and only E-Learning Center in the world today that offers a full range of studies in the field of Chinese Metaphysics.

Convenient

Study from Your Own Home

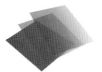

Easy Enrollment

The Mastery Academy's E-Learning Center

Now, armed with your trusty computer or laptop, and Internet access, knowledge of classical Feng Shui, BaZi (Destiny Analysis) and Mian Xiang (Face Reading) are but a literal click away!

Study at your own pace, and interact with your Instructor and fellow students worldwide, from anywhere in the world. With our E-Learning Center, knowledge of Chinese Metaphysics is brought DIRECTLY to you in all its clarity – topic-by-topic, and lesson-by-lesson; with illustrated presentations and comprehensive notes expediting your learning curve!

Your education journey through our E-Learning Center may be done via any of the following approaches:

1. Online Courses

There are 3 Programs available: our Online Feng Shui Program, Online BaZi Program, and Online Mian Xiang Program. Each Program consists of several Levels, with each Level consisting of many Lessons in turn. Each Lesson contains a pre-recorded video session on the topic at hand, accompanied by presentation-slides and graphics as well as downloadable tutorial notes that you can print and file for future reference.

Video Lecture

Presentation Slide

Downloadable Notes

2. MA Live!

MA Live!, as its name implies, enables LIVE broadcasts of Joey Yap's courses and seminars – right to your computer screen. Students will not only get to see and hear Joey talk on real-time `live', but also participate and more importantly, TALK to Joey via the MA Live! interface. All the benefits of a live class, minus the hassle of actually having to attend one!

How It Works 1. 2.

Our Live Classes   You at Home

3. Video-On-Demand (VOD)

Get immediate streaming-downloads of the Mastery Academy's wide range of educational DVDs, right on your computer screen. No more shipping costs and waiting time to be incurred!

Instant VOD Online 1.  2.

Choose From Our list of Available VODs!   Click "Play" on Your PC

Welcome to **www.maelearning.com**; the web portal of our E-Learning Center, and YOUR virtual gateway to Chinese Metaphysics!

Mastery Academy around the world

Canada

United States

Denmark

United Kingdom

Czech Republic

Austria

Switzerland

Netherlands

France

Poland

Germany

Slovenia

Italy

Cyprus

Hungary

Croatia

Greece

Russian Federation

Ukraine

Turkey

Kazakhstan

India

Kuala Lumpur

Malaysia

Philippines

Singapore

Australia

South Africa

New Zealand

YAP GLOBAL CONSULTING

Joey Yap & Yap Global Consulting

Headed by Joey Yap, Yap Global Consulting (YGC) is a leading international consulting firm specializing in Feng Shui, Mian Xiang (Face Reading) and BaZi (Destiny Analysis) consulting services worldwide. Joey - an internationally renowned Master Trainer, Consultant, Speaker and best-selling Author - has dedicated his life to the art and science of Chinese Metaphysics.

YGC has its main offices in Kuala Lumpur and Australia, and draws upon its diverse reservoir of strength from a group of dedicated and experienced consultants based in more than 30 countries, worldwide.

As the pioneer in blending established, classical Chinese Metaphysics techniques with the latest approach in consultation practices, YGC has built its reputation on the principles of professionalism and only the highest standards of service. This allows us to retain the cutting edge in delivering Feng Shui and Destiny consultation services to both corporate and personal clients, in a simple and direct manner, without compromising on quality.

Across Industries: Our Portfolio of Clients

Our diverse portfolio of both corporate and individual clients from all around the world bears testimony to our experience and capabilities.

Virtually every industry imaginable has benefited from our services - ranging from academic and financial institutions, real-estate developers and multinational corporations, to those in the leisure and tourism industry. Our services are also engaged by professionals, prominent business personalities, celebrities, high-profile politicians and people from all walks of life.

YAP GLOBAL CONSULTING

Name (Mr./Mrs./Ms.):_____

Contact Details

Tel:_____ Fax:_____

Mobile :_____

E-mail:_____

What Type of Consultation Are You Interested In?
☐ Feng Shui ☐ BaZi ☐ Date Selection ☐ Yi Jing

Please tick if applicable:
☐ Are you a Property Developer looking to engage Yap Global Consulting?

☐ Are you a Property Investor looking for tailor-made packages to suit your investment requirements?

Please attach your name card here.

Thank you for completing this form. Please fax it back to us at:

Malaysia & the rest of the world
Fax : +603-2284 2213   Tel : +603-2284 1213

www.joeyyap.com

Feng Shui Consultations

For Residential Properties
- Initial Land/Property Assessment
- Residential Feng Shui Consultations
- Residential Land Selection
- End-to-End Residential Consultation

For Commercial Properties
- Initial Land/Property Assessment
- Commercial Feng Shui Consultations
- Commercial Land Selection
- End-to-End Commercial Consultation

For Property Developers
- End-to-End Consultation
- Post-Consultation Advisory Services
- Panel Feng Shui Consultant

For Property Investors
- Your Personal Feng Shui Consultant
- Tailor-Made Packages

For Memorial Parks & Burial Sites
- Yin House Feng Shui

BaZi Consultations

Personal Destiny Analysis
- Personal Destiny Analysis for Individuals
- Children's BaZi Analysis
- Family BaZi Analysis

Strategic Analysis for Corporate Organizations
- Corporate BaZi Consultations
- BaZi Analysis for Human Resource Management

Entrepreneurs & Business Owners
- BaZi Analysis for Entrepreneurs

Career Pursuits
- BaZi Career Analysis

Relationships
- Marriage and Compatibility Analysis
- Partnership Analysis

For Everyone
- Annual BaZi Forecast
- Your Personal BaZi Coach

Date Selection Consultations

- **Marriage Date Selection**
- **Caesarean Birth Date Selection**
- **House-Moving Date Selection**
- **Renovation & Groundbreaking Dates**

- **Signing of Contracts**
- **Official Openings**
- **Product Launches**

Yi Jing Assessment

A Time-Tested, Accurate Science

- With a history predating 4 millennia, the Yi Jing - or Classic of Change - is one of the oldest Chinese texts surviving today. Its purpose as an oracle, in predicting the outcome of things, is based on the variables of Time, Space and Specific Events.

- A Yi Jing Assessment provides specific answers to any specific questions you may have about a specific event or endeavor. This is something that a Destiny Analysis would not be able to give you.

Basically, what a Yi Jing Assessment does is focus on only ONE aspect or item at a particular point in your life, and give you a calculated prediction of the details that will follow suit, if you undertake a particular action. It gives you an insight into a situation, and what course of action to take in order to arrive at a satisfactory outcome at the end of the day.

Please Contact YGC for a personalized Yi Jing Assessment!

Tel: +603-2284 1213   Email: consultation@joeyyap.com

INVITING US TO YOUR CORPORATE EVENTS

Many reputable organizations and institutions have worked closely with YGC to build a synergistic business relationship by engaging our team of consultants, led by Joey Yap, as speakers at their corporate events. Our seminars and short talks are always packed with audiences consisting of clients and associates of multinational and public-listed companies as well as key stakeholders of financial institutions.

We tailor our seminars and talks to suit the anticipated or pertinent group of audience. Be it a department, subsidiary, your clients or even the entire corporation, we aim to fit your requirements in delivering the intended message(s).

CHINESE METAPHYSICS REFERENCE SERIES

The Chinese Metaphysics Reference Series is a collection of reference texts, source material, and educational textbooks to be used as supplementary guides by scholars, students, researchers, teachers and practitioners of Chinese Metaphysics.

These comprehensive and structured books provide fast, easy reference to aid in the study and practice of various Chinese Metaphysics subjects including Feng Shui, BaZi, Yi Jing, Zi Wei, Liu Ren, Ze Ri, Ta Yi, Qi Men and Mian Xiang.

The Chinese Metaphysics Compendium

At over 1,000 pages, the *Chinese Metaphysics Compendium* is a unique one-volume reference book that compiles all the formulas relating to Feng Shui, BaZi (Four Pillars of Destiny), Zi Wei (Purple Star Astrology), Yi Jing (I-Ching), Qi Men (Mystical Doorways), Ze Ri (Date Selection), Mian Xiang (Face Reading) and other sources of Chinese Metaphysics.

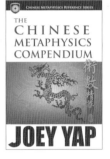

It is presented in the form of easy-to-read tables, diagrams and reference charts, all of which are compiled into one handy book. This first-of-its-kind compendium is presented in both English and the original Chinese, so that none of the meanings and contexts of the technical terminologies are lost.

The only essential and comprehensive reference on Chinese Metaphysics, and an absolute must-have for all students, scholars, and practitioners of Chinese Metaphysics.

Dong Gong Date Selection

Xuan Kong Da Gua Ten Thousand Year Calendar

Xuan Kong Da Gua Reference Book

The Ten Thousand Year Calendar *(Professional Edition)*

The Date Selection Compendium *(Professional Edition)*

Plum Blossoms Divination Reference Book

San Yuan Dragon Gate Eight Formations Water Method

Qi Men Dun Jia 1080 Charts

Earth Study Discern Truth Volume Two

Bazi Structures and Structural Useful Gods - Earth

Bazi Structures and Structural Useful Gods - Fire

Bazi Structures and Structural Useful Gods - Metal

Bazi Structures and Structural Useful Gods - Water

Bazi Structures and Structural Useful Gods - Wood

Educational Tools & Software

Xuan Kong Flying Stars Feng Shui Software
The Essential Application for Enthusiasts and Professionals

The Xuan Kong Flying Stars Feng Shui Software is a brand-new application by Joey Yap that will assist you in the practice of Xuan Kong Feng Shui with minimum fuss and maximum effectiveness. Superimpose the Flying Stars charts over your house plans (or those of your clients) to clearly demarcate the 9 Palaces. Use it to help you create fast and sophisticated chart drawings and presentations, as well as to assist professional practitioners in the report-writing process before presenting the final reports for your clients. Students can use it to practice their Xuan Kong Feng Shui skills and knowledge, and it can even be used by designers and architects!

Some of the highlights of the software include:
- Natal Flying Stars
- Monthly Flying Stars
- 81 Flying Stars Combinations
- Dual-View Format
- Annual Flying Stars
- Flying Stars Integration
- 24 Mountains

All charts will be are printable and configurable, and can be saved for future editing. Also, you'll be able to export your charts into most image file formats like jpeg, bmp, and gif.

The Xuan Kong Flying Stars Feng Shui Software can make your Feng Shui practice simpler and more effective, garnering you amazing results with less effort!

Mini Feng Shui Compass

This Mini Feng Shui Compass with the accompanying Companion Booklet written by leading Feng Shui and Chinese Astrology Master Trainer Joey Yap is a must-have for any Feng Shui enthusiast.

The Mini Feng Shui Compass is a self-aligning compass that is not only light at 100gms but also built sturdily to ensure it will be convenient to use anywhere. The rings on the Mini Feng Shui Compass are bilingual and incorporate the 24 Mountain Rings that is used in your traditional Luo Pan.

The comprehensive booklet included will guide you in applying the 24 Mountain Directions on your Mini Feng Shui Compass effectively and the 8 Mansions Feng Shui to locate the most auspicious locations within your home, office and surroundings. You can also use the Mini Feng Shui Compass when measuring the direction of your property for the purpose of applying Flying Stars Feng Shui.

Educational Tools & Software

BaZi Ming Pan Software Version 2.0
Professional Four Pillars Calculator for Destiny Analysis

The BaZi Ming Pan Version 2.0 Professional Four Pillars Calculator for Destiny Analysis is the most technically advanced software of its kind in the world today. It allows even those without any knowledge of BaZi to generate their own BaZi Charts, and provides virtually every detail required to undertake a comprehensive Destiny Analysis.

This Professional Four Pillars Calculator allows you to even undertake a day-to-day analysis of your Destiny. What's more, all BaZi Charts generated by this software are fully printable and configurable! Designed for both enthusiasts and professional practitioners, this state-of-the-art software blends details with simplicity, and is capable of generating 4 different types of BaZi charts: **BaZi Professional Charts, BaZi Annual Analysis Charts, BaZi Pillar Analysis Charts and BaZi Family Relationship Charts.**

Additional references, configurable to cater to all levels of BaZi knowledge and usage, include:
• Dual Age & Bilingual Option (Western & Chinese) • Na Yin narrations • 12 Life Stages evaluation • Death & Emptiness • Gods & Killings • Special Days • Heavenly Virtue Nobles

This software also comes with a Client Management feature that allows you to save and trace clients' records instantly, navigate effortlessly between BaZi charts, and file your clients' information in an organized manner.

The BaZi Ming Pan Version 2.0 Calculator sets a new standard by combining the best of BaZi and technology.

Joey Yap Feng Shui Template Set

Directions are the cornerstone of any successful Feng Shui audit or application. The **Joey Yap Feng Shui Template Set** is a set of three templates to simplify the process of taking directions and determining locations and positions, whether it's for a building, a house, or an open area such as a plot of land, all with just a floor plan or area map.

The Set comprises 3 basic templates: The Basic Feng Shui Template, 8 Mansions Feng Shui Template, and the Flying Stars Feng Shui Template.

With bi-lingual notations for these directions; both in English and the original Chinese, the **Joey Yap Feng Shui Template Set** comes with its own Booklet that gives simple yet detailed instructions on how to make use of the 3 templates within.

• Easy-to-use, simple, and straightforward
• Small and portable; each template measuring only 5" x 5"
• Additional 8 Mansions and Flying Stars Reference Rings
• Handy companion booklet with usage tips and examples

Accelerate Your Face Reading Skills With Joey Yap's Face Reading Revealed DVD Series

Mian Xiang, the Chinese art of Face Reading, is an ancient form of physiognomy and entails the use of the face and facial characteristics to evaluate key aspects of a person's life, luck and destiny. In his Face Reading DVDs series, Joey Yap shows you how the facial features reveal a wealth of information about a person's luck, destiny and personality.

Mian Xiang also tell us the talents, quirks and personality of an individual. Do you know that just by looking at a person's face, you can ascertain his or her health, wealth, relationships and career? Let Joey Yap show you how the 12 Palaces can be utilised to reveal a person's inner talents, characteristics and much more.

Each facial feature on the face represents one year in a person's life. Your face is a 100-year map of your life and each position reveals your fortune and destiny at a particular age as well as insights and information about your personality, skills, abilities and destiny.

Using Mian Xiang, you will also be able to plan your life ahead by identifying, for example, the right business partner and knowing the sort of person that you need to avoid. By knowing their characteristics through the facial features, you will be able to gauge their intentions and gain an upper hand in negotiations.

Do you know what moles signify? Do they bring good or bad luck? Do you want to build better relationships with your partner or family members or have your ever wondered why you seem to be always bogged down by trivial problems in your life?

In these highly entertaining DVDs, Joey will help you answer all these questions and more. You will be able to ascertain the underlying meaning of moles, birthmarks or even the type of your hair in Face Reading. Joey will also reveal the guidelines to help you foster better and stronger relationships with your loved ones through Mian Xiang.

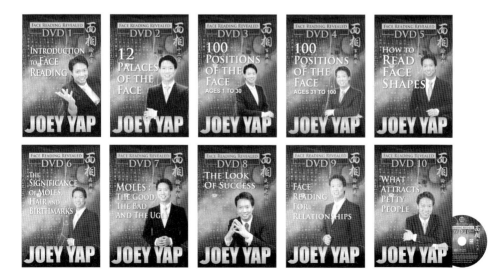

Feng Shui for Homebuyers DVD Series

Best-selling Author, and international Master Trainer and Consultant Joey Yap reveals in these DVDs the significant Feng Shui features that every homebuyer should know when evaluating a property.

Joey will guide you on how to customise your home to maximise the Feng Shui potential of your property and gain the full benefit of improving your health, wealth and love life using the 9 Palace Grid. He will show you how to go about applying the classical applications of the Life Gua and House Gua techniques to get attuned to your Sheng Qi (positive energies).

In these DVDs, you will also learn how to identify properties with good Feng Shui features that will help you promote a fulfilling life and achieve your full potential. Discover how to avoid properties with negative Feng Shui that can bring about detrimental effects to your health, wealth and relationships.

Joey will also elaborate on how to fix the various aspects of your home that may have an impact on the Feng Shui of your property and give pointers on how to tap into the positive energies to support your goals.

Discover Feng Shui with Joey Yap (TV Series)

Discover Feng Shui with Joey Yap: Set of 4 DVDs

Informative and entertaining, classical Feng Shui comes alive in *Discover Feng Shui with Joey Yap!*

Dying to know how you can use Feng Shui to improve your house or office, but simply too busy attend for formal classes?

You have the questions. Now let Joey personally answer them in this 4-set DVD compilation! Learn how to ensure the viability of your residence or workplace, Feng Shui-wise, without having to convert it into a Chinese antiques' shop. Classical Feng Shui is about harnessing the natural power of your environment to improve quality of life. It's a systematic and subtle metaphysical science.

And that's not all. Joey also debunks many a myth about classical Feng Shui, and shares with viewers Face Reading tips as well!

Own the series that national channel 8TV did a re-run of in 2005, today!

Continue Your Journey with Joey Yap's Books

Pure Feng Shui

Pure Feng Shui is Joey Yap's debut with an international publisher, and is a refreshing and elegant look at the intricacies of Classical Feng Shui – now compiled in a useful manner for modern-day readers. This book is a comprehensive introduction to all the important precepts and techniques of Feng Shui practice.

He reveals how to use Feng Shui to bring prosperity, good relationships, and success into one's life the simple and genuine way – without having to resort to symbols or figurines! He shows readers how to work with what they have and make simple and sustainable changes that can have significant Feng Shui effect. The principles of Classical Feng Shui and Chinese Astrology inform his teachings and explanations, so all that the readers need are a compass, a pencil, some paper, and an open mind!

Joey Yap's Art of Face Reading

The Art of Face Reading is Joey Yap's second effort with an international publisher, and takes a lighter, more practical approach to Face Reading. This book does not so much focus on the individual features as it does on reading the entire face. It is about identifying common personality types and characters.

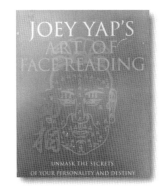

Joey shows readers how to identify successful career faces, or faces that are most likely to be able to do well financially. He also explores Face Reading in the context of health. He uses examples of real people - famous and ordinary folk - to allow readers to better understand what these facial features look like on an actual face. Readers will learn how to identify faces in Career, Wealth, Relationships, and Health (eg. 'The Salesperson Face,' 'The Politician Face,' 'The Unfaithful One,' 'The Shopaholic One,' and plenty more.)

Continue Your Journey with Joey Yap's Books

Easy Guide on Face Reading

The Face Reading Essentials series of books comprise 5 individual books on the key features of the face – Eyes, Eyebrows, Ears, Nose, and Mouth. Each book provides a detailed illustration and a simple yet descriptive explanation on the individual types of the features.

The books are equally useful and effective for beginners, enthusiasts, and the curious. The series is designed to enable people who are new to Face Reading to make the most of first impressions and learn to apply Face Reading skills to understand the personality and character of friends, family, co-workers, and even business associates.

  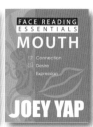 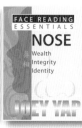 

BaZi Essentials Series

The BaZi Essentials series of books comprise 10 individual books that focus on the individual Day Masters in BaZi (Four Pillars of Destiny, or Chinese Astrology) study and analysis. With each book focusing on one particular Day Master, Joey explains why the Day Master is the fundamental starting point for BaZi analysis, and is the true essence of one's character traits and basic identity.

With these concise and entertaining books that are designed to be both informative and entertaining, Joey shows how each person is different and unique, yet share similar traits, according to his or her respective Day Master. These 10 guides will provide crucial insight into why people behave in the various different ways they do.

 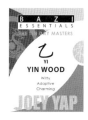   

Continue Your Journey with Joey Yap's Books

Walking the Dragons

Walking the Dragons is a guided tour through the classical landform Feng Shui of ancient China, an enchanting collection of deeply-researched yet entertaining essays rich in historical detail.

Compiled in one book for the first time from Joey Yap's Feng Shui Mastery Excursion Series, the book highlights China's extensive, vibrant history with astute observations on the Feng Shui of important sites and places. Learn the landform formations of Yin Houses (tombs and burial places), as well as mountains, temples, castles, and villages.

It demonstrates complex Feng Shui theories and principles in easy-to-understand, entertaining language and is the perfect addition to the bookshelf of a Feng Shui or history lover. Anyone, whether experienced in Feng Shui or new to the practice, will be able to enjoy the insights shared in this book. Complete with gorgeous full-colour pictures of all the amazing sights and scenery, it's the next best thing to having been there yourself!

Your Aquarium Here

Your Aquarium Here is a simple, practical, hands-on Feng Shui book that teaches you how to incorporate a Water feature – an aquarium – for optimal Feng Shui benefit, whether for personal relationships, wealth, or career. Designed to be comprehensive yet simple enough for a novice or beginner, *Your Aquarium Here* provides historical and factual information about the role of Water in Feng Shui, and provides a step-by-step guide to installing and using an aquarium.

The book is the first in the **Fengshuilogy Series**, a series of matter-of-fact and useful Feng Shui books designed for the person who wants to do fuss-free Feng Shui. Not everyone who wants to use Feng Shui is an expert or a scholar! This series of books are just the kind you'd want on your bookshelf to gain basic, practical knowledge of the subject. Go ahead and Feng Shui-It-Yourself – *Your Aquarium Here* eliminates all the fuss and bother, but maintains all the fun and excitement, of authentic Feng Shui application!

The Art of Date Selection: Personal Date Selection

In today's modern world, it is not good enough to just do things effectively – we need to do them efficiently, as well. From the signing of business contracts and moving into a new home, to launching a product or even tying the knot; everything has to move, and move very quickly too. There is a premium on Time, where mistakes can indeed be costly.

The notion of doing the Right Thing, at the Right Time and in the Right Place is the very backbone of Date Selection. Because by selecting a suitable date specially tailored to a specific activity or endeavor, we infuse it with the most positive energies prevalent in our environment during that particular point in time; and that could well make the difference between `make-and-break'! With the *Art of Date Selection: Personal Date Selection*, learn simple, practical methods you can employ to select not just good dates, but personalized good dates. Whether it's a personal activity such as a marriage or professional endeavor such as launching a business, signing a contract or even acquiring assets, this book will show you how to pick the good dates and tailor them to suit the activity in question, as well as avoid the negative ones too!

The Art of Date Selection: Feng Shui Date Selection

Date Selection is the Art of selecting the most suitable date, where the energies present on the day support the specific activities or endeavors we choose to undertake on that day. Feng Shui is the Chinese Metaphysical study of the Physiognomy of the Land – landforms and the Qi they produce, circulate and conduct. Hence, anything that exists on this Earth is invariably subject to the laws of Feng Shui. So what do we get when Date Selection and Feng Shui converge?

Feng Shui Date Selection, of course! Say you wish to renovate your home, or maybe buy or rent one. Or perhaps, you're a developer, and wish to know WHEN is the best date possible to commence construction works on your project. In any case – and all cases – you certainly wish to ensure that your endeavors are well supported by the positive energies present on a good day, won't you? And this is where Date Selection supplements the practice of Feng Shui. At the end of the day, it's all about making the most of what's good, and minimizing what's bad.

(Available Soon)

Continue Your Journey with Joey Yap's Books

Feng Shui For Homebuyers - Exterior (English & Chinese versions)

Best selling Author and international Feng Shui Consultant, Joey Yap, will guide you on the various important features in your external environment that have a bearing on the Feng Shui of your home. For homeowners, those looking to build their own home or even investors who are looking to apply Feng Shui to their homes, this book provides valuable information from the classical Feng Shui theories and applications.

This book will assist you in screening and eliminating unsuitable options with negative FSQ (Feng Shui Quotient) should you acquire your own land or if you are purchasing a newly built home. It will also help you in determining which plot of land to select and which to avoid when purchasing an empty parcel of land.

Feng Shui for Homebuyers - Interior

A book every homeowner or potential house buyer should have. The Feng Shui for Homebuyers (Interior) is an informative reference book and invaluable guide written by best selling Author and international Feng Shui Consultant, Joey Yap.

This book provides answers to the important questions of what really does matter when looking at the internal Feng Shui of a home or office. It teaches you how to analyze your home or office floor plans and how to improve their Feng Shui. It will answer all your questions about the positive and negative flow of Qi within your home and ways to utilize them to your maximum benefit.

Providing you with a guide to calculating your Life Gua and House Gua to fine-tune your Feng Shui within your property, Joey Yap focuses on practical, easily applicable ideas on what you can implement internally in a property.

Feng Shui for Apartment Buyers - Home Owners

Finding a good apartment or condominium is never an easy task but who do you ensure that is also has good Feng Shui? And how exactly do you apply Feng Shui to an apartment or condominium or high-rise residence?

These questions and more are answered by renowned Feng Shui Consultant and Master Trainer Joey Yap in **Feng Shui for Apartment Buyers - Home Owners**. Joey answers the key questions about Feng Shui and apartments, then guides you through the bare basics like taking a direction and super-imposing a Flying Stars chart onto a floor plan. Joey also walks you through the process of finding an apartment with favorable Feng Shui, sharing with you some of the key methods and techniques that are employed by professional Feng Shui consultants in assesing apartment Feng Shui.

In his trademark straight-to-the-point manner, Joey shares with you the Feng Shui do's and dont's when it comes to finding an apartment with favorable Feng Shui and which is conducive for home living.

The Ten Thousand Year Calendar

The Ten Thousand Year Calendar or 萬年曆 Wan Nian Li is a regular reference book and an invaluable tool used by masters, practitioners and students of Feng Shui, BaZi (Four Pillars of Destiny), Chinese Zi Wei Dou Shu Astrology (Purple Star), Yi Jing (I-Ching) and Date Selection specialists.

JOEY YAP's *Ten Thousand Year Calendar* provides the Gregorian (Western) dates converted into both the Chinese Solar and Lunar calendar in both the English and Chinese language.

It also includes a comprehensive set of key Feng Shui and Chinese Astrology charts and references, including Xuan Kong Nine Palace Flying Star Charts, Monthly and Daily Flying Stars, Water Dragon Formulas Reference Charts, Zi Wei Dou Shu (Purple Star) Astrology Reference Charts, BaZi (Four Pillars of Destiny) Heavenly Stems, Earthly Branches and all other related reference tables for Chinese Metaphysical Studies.

Continue Your Journey with Joey Yap's Books

Stories and Lessons on Feng Shui (English & Chinese versions)

Stories and Lessons on Feng Shui is a compilation of essays and stories written by leading Feng Shui and Chinese Astrology trainer and consultant Joey Yap about Feng Shui and Chinese Astrology.

In this heart-warming collection of easy to read stories, find out why it's a myth that you should never have Water on the right hand side of your house, the truth behind the infamous 'love' and 'wealth' corners and that the sudden death of a pet fish is really NOT due to bad luck!

More Stories and Lessons on Feng Shui

Finally, the long-awaited sequel to *Stories & Lessons on Feng Shui*!

If you've read the best-selling Stories & Lessons on Feng Shui, you won't want to miss this book. And even if you haven't read *Stories & Lessons on Feng Shui*, there's always a time to rev your Feng Shui engine up.

The time is NOW.

And the book? *More Stories & Lessons on Feng Shui* – the 2nd compilation of the most popular articles and columns penned by Joey Yap; **specially featured in national and international publications, magazines and newspapers.**

All in all, *More Stories & Lessons on Feng Shui* is a delightful chronicle of Joey's articles, thoughts and vast experience - as a professional Feng Shui consultant and instructor - that have been purposely refined, edited and expanded upon to make for a light-hearted, interesting yet educational read. And with Feng Shui, BaZi, Mian Xiang and Yi Jing all thrown into this one dish, there's something for everyone…so all you need to serve or accompany *More Stories & Lessons on Feng Shui* with is your favorite cup of tea or coffee!

Even More Stories and Lessons on Feng Shui

In this third release in the Stories and Lessons series, Joey Yap continues his exploration on the study and practice of Feng Shui in the modern age through a series of essays and personal anecdotes. Debunking superstition, offering simple and understandable "Feng Shui-It-Yourself" tips, and expounding on the history and origins of classical Feng Shui, Joey takes readers on a journey that is always refreshing and exciting.

Besides 'behind-the-scenes' revelations of actual Feng Shui audits, there are also chapters on how beginners can easily and accurately incorporate Feng Shui practice into their lives, as well as travel articles that offer proof that when it comes to Feng Shui, the Qi literally knows no boundaries.

In his trademark lucid and forthright style, Joey covers themes and topics that will strike a chord with all readers who have an interest in Feng Shui.

Mian Xiang - Discover Face Reading (English & Chinese versions)

Need to identify a suitable business partner? How about understanding your staff or superiors better? Or even choosing a suitable spouse? These mind boggling questions can be answered in Joey Yap's introductory book to Face Reading titled *Mian Xiang – Discover Face Reading*. This book will help you discover the hidden secrets in a person's face.

Mian Xiang – Discover Face Reading is comprehensive book on all areas of Face Reading, covering some of the most important facial features, including the forehead, mouth, ears and even the philtrum above your lips. This book will help you analyse not just your Destiny but help you achieve your full potential and achieve life fulfillment.

Continue Your Journey with Joey Yap's Books

BaZi - The Destiny Code (English & Chinese versions)

Leading Chinese Astrology Master Trainer Joey Yap makes it easy to learn how to unlock your Destiny through your BaZi with this book. BaZi or Four Pillars of Destiny is an ancient Chinese science which enables individuals to understand their personality, hidden talents and abilities as well as their luck cycle, simply by examining the information contained within their birth data. *The Destiny Code* is the first book that shows readers how to plot and interpret their own Destiny Charts and lays the foundation for more in-depth BaZi studies. Written in a lively entertaining style, the Destiny Code makes BaZi accessible to the layperson. Within 10 chapters, understand and appreciate more about this astoundingly accurate ancient Chinese Metaphysical science.

BaZi - The Destiny Code Revealed

In this follow up to Joey Yap's best-selling *The Destiny Code*, delve deeper into your own Destiny chart through an understanding of the key elemental relationships that affect the Heavenly Stems and Earthly Branches. Find out how Combinations, Clash, Harm, Destructions and Punishments bring new dimension to a BaZi chart. Complemented by extensive real-life examples, *The Destiny Code Revealed* takes you to the next level of BaZi, showing you how to unlock the Codes of Destiny and to take decisive action at the right time, and capitalise on the opportunities in life.

Xuan Kong: Flying Stars Feng Shui

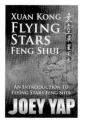

Xuan Kong Flying Stars Feng Shui is an essential introductory book to the subject of Xuan Kong Fei Xing, a well-known and popular system of Feng Shui, written by International Feng Shui Master Trainer Joey Yap.

In his down-to-earth, entertaining and easy to read style, Joey Yap takes you through the essential basics of Classical Feng Shui, and the key concepts of Xuan Kong Fei Xing (Flying Stars). Learn how to fly the stars, plot a Flying Star chart for your home or office and interpret the stars and star combinations. Find out how to utilise the favourable areas of your home or office for maximum benefit and learn 'tricks of the trade' and 'trade secrets' used by Feng Shui practitioners to enhance and maximise Qi in your home or office.

An essential integral introduction to the subject of Classical Feng Shui and the Flying Stars System of Feng Shui!

Xuan Kong Flying Stars: Structures and Combinations

Delve deeper into Flying Stars through a greater understanding of the 81 Combinations and the influence of the Annual and Monthly Stars on the Base, Sitting and Facing Stars in this 2nd book in the Xuan Kong Feng Shui series. Learn how Structures like the Combination of 10, Up the Mountain and Down the River, Pearl and Parent String Structures are used to interpret a Flying Star chart.

(Available Soon)

Xuan Kong Flying Stars: Advanced Techniques

Take your knowledge of Xuan Kong Flying Stars to a higher level and learn how to apply complex techniques and advanced formulas such as Castle Gate Technique, Seven Star Robbery Formation, Advancing the Dragon Formation and Replacement Star technique amongst others. Joey Yap also shows you how to use the Life Palace technique to combine Gua Numbers with Flying Star numbers and utilise the predictive facets of Flying Stars Feng Shui.

(Available Soon)

Annual Releases

Chinese Astrology for 2010

This information-packed annual guide to the Chinese Astrology for 2010 goes way beyond the conventional `animal horoscope' book. To begin with, author Joey Yap includes a personalized outlook for 2010 based on the individual's BaZi Day Pillar (Jia Zi) and a 12-month micro-analysis for each of the 60 Day Pillars – in addition to the annual outlook for all 12 animal signs and the 12-month outlook for each animal sign in 2010. Find out what awaits you in 2010 from the four key aspects of Health, Wealth, Career and Relationships…with Joey Yap's **Chinese Astrology for 2010**!

Feng Shui for 2010

Maximize the Qi of the Year of the Metal Tiger for your home and office, with Joey Yap's **Feng Shui for 2010** book. Learn how to tap into the positive sectors of the year, and avoid the negative ones and those with the Annual Afflictions, as well as ascertain how the annual Flying Stars affect your property by comparing them against the Eight Mansions (Ba Zhai) for 2010. Flying Stars enthusiasts will also find this book handy, as it includes the monthly Flying Stars charts for the year, accompanied by detailed commentaries on what sectors to use and avoid – to enable you to optimize your Academic, Relationships and Wealth Luck in 2010.

Weekly Tong Shu Diary 2010

Organize your professional and personal lives with the **Tong Shu Diary 2010**, with a twist… it also allows you to determine the most suitable dates on which you can undertake important activities and endeavors throughout the year! This compact Diary integrates the Chinese Solar and Lunar Calendars with the universal lingua franca of the Gregorian Calendar.

Tong Shu Monthly Planner 2010

Tailor-made for the Feng Shui or BaZi enthusiast in you, or even professional Chinese Metaphysics consultants who want a compact planner with useful information incorporated into it. In the **Tong Shu Monthly Planner 2010**, you will find the auspicious and inauspicious dates for the year marked out for you, alongside the most suitable activities to be undertaken on each day. As a bonus, there is also a reference section containing all the monthly Flying Stars charts and Annual Afflictions for 2010.

Tong Shu Desktop Calendar 2010

Get an instant snapshot of the suitable and unsuitable activities for each day of the Year of the Earth Rat, with the icons displayed on this lightweight Desktop Calendar. Elegantly presenting the details of the Chinese Solar Calendar in the form of the standard Gregorian one, the **Tong Shu Desktop Calendar 2010** is perfect for Chinese Metaphysics enthusiasts and practitioners alike. Whether it a business launching or meeting, ground breaking ceremony, travel or house-moving that you have in mind, this Calendar is designed to fulfill your information needs.

Tong Shu Year Planner 2010

This one-piece Planner presents you all the essential information you need for significant activities or endeavors…with just a quick glance! In a nutshell, it allows you to identify the favorable and unfavorable days, which will in turn enable you to schedule your year's activities so as to make the most of good days, and avoid the ill-effects brought about by inauspicious ones.

Elevate Your Feng Shui Skills With Joey Yap's Home Study Course And Educational DVDs

Xuan Kong Vol.1
An Advanced Feng Shui Home Study Course

Learn the Xuan Kong Flying Star Feng Shui system in just 20 lessons! Joey Yap's specialised notes and course work have been written to enable distance learning without compromising on the breadth or quality of the syllabus. Learn at your own pace with the same material students in a live class would use. The most comprehensive distance learning course on Xuan Kong Flying Star Feng Shui in the market. Xuan Kong Flying Star Vol.1 comes complete with a special binder for all your course notes.

Feng Shui for Period 8 - (DVD)

Don't miss the Feng Shui Event of the next 20 years! Catch Joey Yap LIVE and find out just what Period 8 is all about. This DVD boxed set zips you through the fundamentals of Feng Shui and the impact of this important change in the Feng Shui calendar. Joey's entertaining, conversational style walks you through the key changes that Period 8 will bring and how to tap into Wealth Qi and Good Feng Shui for the next 20 years.

Xuan Kong Flying Stars Beginners Workshop - (DVD)

Take a front row seat in Joey Yap's Xuan Kong Flying Stars workshop with this unique LIVE RECORDING of Joey Yap's Xuan Kong Flying Stars Feng Shui workshop, attended by over 500 people. This DVD program provides an effective and quick introduction of Xuan Kong Feng Shui essentials for those who are just starting out in their study of classical Feng Shui. Learn to plot your own Flying Star chart in just 3 hours. Learn 'trade secret' methods, remedies and cures for Flying Stars Feng Shui. This boxed set contains 3 DVDs and 1 workbook with notes and charts for reference.

BaZi Four Pillars of Destiny Beginners Workshop - (DVD)

Ever wondered what Destiny has in store for you? Or curious to know how you can learn more about your personality and inner talents? BaZi or Four Pillars of Destiny is an ancient Chinese science that enables us to understand a person's hidden talent, inner potential, personality, health and wealth luck from just their birth data. This specially compiled DVD set of Joey Yap's BaZi Beginners Workshop provides a thorough and comprehensive introduction to BaZi. Learn how to read your own chart and understand your own luck cycle. This boxed set contains 3 DVDs and 1 workbook with notes and reference charts.

Interested in learning MORE about Feng Shui? Advance Your Feng Shui Knowledge with the Mastery Academy Courses.

Feng Shui Mastery Series™
LIVE COURSES (MODULES ONE TO FOUR)

Feng Shui Mastery – Module One
Beginners Course

Designed for students seeking an entry-level intensive program into the study of Feng Shui , Module One is an intensive foundation course that aims not only to provide you with an introduction to Feng Shui theories and formulas and equip you with the skills and judgments to begin practicing and conduct simple Feng Shui audits upon successful completion of the course. Learn all about Forms, Eight Mansions Feng Shui and Flying Star Feng Shui in just one day with a unique, structured learning program that makes learning Feng Shui quick and easy!

Feng Shui Mastery – Module Two
Practitioners Course

Building on the knowledge and foundation in classical Feng Shui theory garnered in M1, M2 provides a more advanced and in-depth understanding of Eight Mansions, Xuan Kong Flying Star and San He and introduces students to theories that are found only in the classical Chinese Feng Shui texts. This 3-Day Intensive course hones analytical and judgment skills, refines Luo Pan (Chinese Feng Shui compass) skills and reveals 'trade secret' remedies. Module Two covers advanced Forms Analysis, San He's Five Ghost Carry Treasure formula, Advanced Eight Mansions and Xuan Kong Flying Stars and equips you with the skills needed to undertake audits and consultations for residences and offices.

Feng Shui Mastery – Module Three
Advanced Practitioners Course

Module Three is designed for Professional Feng Shui Practitioners. Learn advanced topics in Feng Shui and take your skills to a cutting edge level. Be equipped with the knowledge, techniques and confidence to conduct large scale audits (like estate and resort planning). Learn how to apply different systems appropriately to remedy situations or cases deemed inauspicious by one system and reconcile conflicts in different systems of Feng Shui. Gain advanced knowledge of San He (Three Harmony) systems and San Yuan (Three Cycles) systems, advanced Luan Tou (Forms Feng Shui) and specialist Water Formulas.

Feng Shui Mastery – Module Four
Master Course

The graduating course of the Feng Shui Mastery (FSM) Series, this course takes the advanced practitioner to the Master level. Power packed M4 trains students to 'walk the mountains' and identify superior landform, superior grade structures and make qualitative evaluations of landform, structures, Water and Qi and covers advanced and exclusive topics of San He, San Yuan, Xuan Kong, Ba Zhai, Luan Tou (Advanced Forms and Water Formula) Feng Shui. Master Internal, External and Luan Tou (Landform) Feng Shui methodologies to apply Feng Shui at every level and undertake consultations of every scale and magnitude, from houses and apartments to housing estates, townships, shopping malls and commercial districts.

BaZi Mastery Series™
LIVE COURSES (MODULES ONE TO FOUR)

BaZi Mastery – Module One
Intensive Foundation Course

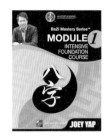

This Intensive One Day Foundation Course provides an introduction to the principles and fundamentals of BaZi (Four Pillars of Destiny) and Destiny Analysis methods such as Ten Gods, Useful God and Strength of Qi. Learn how to plot a BaZi chart and interpret your Destiny and your potential. Master BaZi and learn to capitalize on your strengths, minimize risks and downturns and take charge of your Destiny.

BaZi Mastery – Module Two
Practitioners Course

BaZi Module Two teaches students advanced BaZi analysis techniques and specific analysis methods for relationship luck, health evaluation, wealth potential and career potential. Students will learn to identify BaZi chart structures, sophisticated methods for applying the Ten Gods, and how to read Auxiliary Stars. Students who have completed Module Two will be able to conduct professional BaZi readings.

BaZi Mastery – Module Three
Advanced Practitioners Program

Designed for the BaZi practitioner, learn how to read complex cases and unique events in BaZi charts and perform Big and Small assessments. Discover how to analyze personalities and evaluate talents precisely, as well as special formulas and classical methodologies for BaZi from classics such as Di Tian Sui and Qiong Tong Bao Jian.

BaZi Mastery – Module Four
Master Course in BaZi

The graduating course of the BaZi Mastery Series, this course takes the advanced practitioner to the Masters' level. BaZi M4 focuses on specialized techniques of BaZi reading, unique special structures and advance methods from ancient classical texts. This program includes techniques on date selection and ancient methodologies from the Qiong Tong Bao Jian and Yuan Hai Zi Ping classics.

Xuan Kong Mastery – Module One
Advanced Foundation Program

This course is for the experienced Feng Shui professionals who wish to expand their knowledge and skills in the Xuan Kong system of Feng Shui, covering important foundation methods and techniques from the Wu Chang and Guang Dong lineages of Xuan Kong Feng Shui.

Xuan Kong Mastery – Module Two A
Advanced Xuan Kong Methodologies

Designed for Feng Shui practitioners seeking to specialise in the Xuan Kong system, this program focuses on methods of application and Joey Yap's unique Life Palace and Shifting Palace Methods, as well as methods and techniques from the Wu Chang lineage.

Xuan Kong Mastery – Module Two B
Purple White

Explore in detail and in great depth the star combinations in Xuan Kong. Learn how each different combination reacts or responds in different palaces, under different environmental circumstances and to whom in the property. Learn methods, theories and techniques extracted from ancient classics such as Xuan Kong Mi Zhi, Xuan Kong Fu, Fei Xing Fu and Zi Bai Jue.

Xuan Kong Mastery – Module Three
Advanced Xuan Kong Da Gua

This intensive course focuses solely on the Xuan Kong Da Gua system covering the theories, techniques and methods of application of this unique 64-Hexagram based system of Xuan Kong including Xuan Kong Da Gua for landform analysis.

Walk the Mountains! Learn Feng Shui in a Practical and Hands-on Program

Feng Shui Mastery Excursion Series™ : CHINA

Learn landform (Luan Tou) Feng Shui by walking the mountains and chasing the Dragon's vein in China. This Program takes the students in a study tour to examine notable Feng Shui landmarks, mountains, hills, valleys, ancient palaces, famous mansions, houses and tombs in China. The Excursion is a 'practical' hands-on course where students are shown to perform readings using the formulas they've learnt and to recognize and read Feng Shui Landform (Luan Tou) formations.

Read about China Excursion here:
http://www.masteryacademy.com/Education/schoolfengshui/fengshuimasteryexcursion.asp

Mian Xiang Mastery Series™
LIVE COURSES (MODULES ONE AND TWO)

Mian Xiang Mastery – Module One
Basic Face Reading

A person's face is their fortune – learn more about the ancient Chinese art of Face Reading. In just one day, be equipped with techniques and skills to read a person's face and ascertain their character, luck, wealth and relationship luck.

Mian Xiang Mastery – Module Two
Practical Face Reading

Mian Xiang Module Two covers face reading techniques extracted from the ancient classics Shen Xiang Quan Pian and Shen Xiang Tie Guan Dau. Gain a greater depth and understanding of Mian Xiang and learn to recognize key structures and characteristics in a person's face.

Yi Jing Mastery Series™
LIVE COURSES (MODULES ONE AND TWO)

Yi Jing Mastery – Module One
Traditional Yi Jing

'Yi', relates to change. Change is the only constant in life and the universe, without exception to this rule. The Yi Jing is hence popularly referred to as the Book or Classic of Change. Discoursed in the language of Yin and Yang, the Yi Jing is one of the oldest Chinese classical texts surviving today. With Traditional Yi Jing, learnn how this Classic is used to divine the outcomes of virtually every facet of life; from your relationships to seeking an answer to the issues you may face in your daily life.

Yi Jing Mastery – Module Two
Plum Blossom Numerology

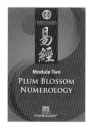

Shao Yong, widely regarded as one of the greatest scholars of the Sung Dynasty, developed Mei Hua Yi Shu (Plum Blossom Numerology) as a more advanced means for divination purpose using the Yi Jing. In Plum Blossom Numerology, the results of a hexagram are interpreted by referring to the Gua meanings, where the interaction and relationship between the five elements, stems, branches and time are equally taken into consideration. This divination method, properly applied, allows us to make proper decisions whenever we find ourselves in a predicament.

Ze Ri Mastery Series™
LIVE COURSES (MODULES ONE AND TWO)

Ze Ri Mastery Series Module 1
Personal and Feng Shui Date Selection

The Mastery Academy's Date Selection Mastery Series Module 1 is specifically structured to provide novice students with an exciting introduction to the Art of Date Selection. Learn the rudiments and tenets of this intriguing metaphysical science. What makes a good date, and what makes a bad date? What dates are suitable for which activities, and what dates simply aren't? And of course, the mother of all questions: WHY aren't all dates created equal. All in only one Module – Module 1!

Ze Ri Mastery Series Module 2
Xuan Kong Da Gua Date Selection

In Module 2, discover advanced Date Selection techniques that will take your knowledge of this Art to a level equivalent to that of a professional's! This is the Module where Date Selection infuses knowledge of the ancient metaphysical science of Feng Shui and BaZi (Chinese Astrology, or Four Pillars of Destiny). Feng Shui, as a means of maximizing Human Luck (i.e. our luck on Earth), is often quoted as the cure to BaZi, which allows us to decipher our Heaven (i.e. inherent) Luck. And one of the most potent ways of making the most of what life has to offer us is to understand our Destiny, know how we can use the natural energies of our environment for our environments and MOST importantly, WHEN we should use these energies and for WHAT endeavors!

You will learn specific methods on how to select suitable dates, tailored to specific activities and events. More importantly, you will also be taught how to suit dates to a person's BaZi (Chinese Astrology, or Four Pillars of Destiny), in order to maximize his or her strengths, and allow this person to surmount any challenges that lie in wait. Add in the factor of `place', and you would have satisfied the notion of `doing the right thing, at the right time and in the right place'! A basic knowledge of BaZi and Feng Shui will come in handy in this Module, although these are not pre-requisites to successfully undergo Module 2.

Feng Shui for Life

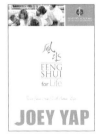

Feng Shui for life is a 5-day course designed for the Feng Shui beginner to learn how to apply practical Feng Shui in day-to-day living. It is a culmination of powerful tools and techniques that allows you to gain quick proficiency in Classical Feng Shui. Discover quick tips on analysing your own BaZi, how to apply Feng Shui solutions for your own home, how to select auspicious dates for important activities, as well as simple and useful Face Reading techniques and practical Water Formulas. This is a complete beginner's course that is suitable for anyone with an interest in applying practical, real-world Feng Shui for life! Enhance every aspect of your life – your health, wealth, and relationships – using these easy-to-apply Classical Feng Shui methods.

Mastery Academy courses are conducted around the world. Find out when will Joey Yap be in your area by visiting **www.masteryacademy.com** or call our office at **+603-2284 8080**.